RIVER OUSE
BARGEMAN

RIVER OUSE BARGEMAN

A LIFE ON THE YORKSHIRE OUSE

by
DAVID LEWIS

PEN & SWORD
TRANSPORT

WHY IS A SHIP LIKE A WOMAN?

This book describes the life and times of a Selby bargeman, Laurie Dews.
As with all bargemen, he had to know about the important details in life.
Two of the most significant of these are your partner and your workplace.
This little passage shows the inextricable links between the two.

A ship is like a woman because...

- In port there is always a bustle around her, and a gang of men too

- She has a waist and stays and it takes a lot of paint to keep her good looking

- It's not the initial expense but the cost of upkeep that breaks you

- When she's all decked out, it takes a good man to handle her

- She shows off her topsides, but hides her bottom

- And when going into port always heads for the buoys.

First published in Great Britain in 2017 by
Pen & Sword Transport
An imprint of Pen & Sword Books Ltd
47 Church Street, Barnsley, South Yorkshire S70 2AS

ISBN PB 978 1 5267 165 90 ISBN HB 978 1 473 880 696

 Pen & Sword Books Ltd incorporates the imprints of Pen & Sword
Archaeology, Atlas, Aviation, Battleground, Discovery, Family History,
History, Maritime, Military, Naval, Politics, Railways, Select, Social History,
Transport, True Crime, and Claymore Press, Frontline Books, Leo Cooper,
Praetorian Press, Remember When, Seaforth Publishing and Wharncliffe.

For a complete list of Pen & Sword titles please contact
Pen & Sword Books Limited
47 Church Street, Barnsley, South Yorkshire S70 2AS England
E-mail: enquiries@pen-and-sword.co.uk
Website: www.pen-and-sword.co.uk

Design and typesetting
by Juliet Arthur, www.stimula.co.uk

Printed and bound by Replika Press Pvt. Ltd.

CONTENTS

INTRODUCTION

The picture shows a man at ease with the world. It's a sunny day, he's in the bridgehouse of his barge, on a river he has worked all his adult life, doing a job his family has followed for over a century.

This gentleman is Laurence 'Laurie' Dews, and this book is the story of his family, his working life and of a way of earning a living that had existed for centuries, but at the time the picture was taken in 1986 was waning, and now, by 2016, has vanished forever.

Laurie was part of a team that worked for the seed-crushing mills at Barlby near Selby on the River Ouse. The mills were established by Joseph Watson of Venus Soap fame, just before the First World War. Watson had a fleet of unpowered or 'dumb' barges built and hired a group of bargees to work for him carrying cargoes from vessels moored in the docks in Hull.

Laurie Dews in the wheelhouse of the *Selby Margaret* on the River Ouse, 1986.
(Laurie Dews)

Laurie's father and grandfather worked on these barges, and Laurie began his work on the river on these craft in the late 1930s. After wartime experience, Laurie returned to the river, and as the 1950s wore on, dumb barges were replaced by powered craft. By 1960, Laurie was experienced enough to become skipper of one of these.

The trade continued much as before throughout the Sixties, but as time wore on, improvements in transport technology meant that fewer seed-carrying craft docked at Hull, and those craft that did dock along the river had their cargoes carried away in larger lorries on more freight-friendly roads.

At the start of the 1980s, the life-expired powered barges were not replaced, and the corps of bargemen were paid off. Laurie and his mates were found jobs ashore until retirement beckoned in 1987. This last generation of bargemen had a huge store of knowledge and know-how to enable them to pilot their craft along the testing shoals and sandbars of the Ouse, the toughness and dexterity to handle 10-inch diameter hemp ropes, anchors with 100 feet of chain attached and twenty-foot-long boat hooks to manoeuvre their craft, and the physical strength to shovel 200 tons of seed into waiting bucket elevators. And when they had done that once, trek back down river to do it all again.

Since 1987, all of Laurie's fellow skippers have 'fallen off the hook' – to use the bargees' euphemism for dying – and Laurie is the proudly proclaimed 'Last of the River Bargemen' to tell the bargemen's stories and to pass on that knowledge. This book, therefore, is a combination of both Laurie's first-hand accounts and some factual exposition and expansion of some of the points he raises. Throughout the book, Laurie's recollections are in italics, the exposition in plain text.

Where do I, as editor, come into this story? In 2008, I began a contract with Groundwork North Yorkshire, working under guidelines formulated by the Heritage Lottery Fund and local Councils to unearth and popularize what was described as the 'Hidden Heritage of Selby'. Part of the remit was to record the personal stories of people who had worked in one of Selby's former industries, not only the barge trade, but also manufacturing, agriculture and transport. I first met Laurie in 2010 and since then have had the great privilege of learning about his life and times, enjoying his wonderfully generous personality, and laughing at his anecdotes and saucy songs.

It is therefore a great pleasure to be able to try to put down Laurie's wit and wisdom in a form that allows others to have a taste of a lost way of life. I am hugely grateful to Laurie for sharing his wit and wisdom with me and patiently explaining that which I did not grasp at first hearing. I have grown to love his ability to spin a yarn. Those yarns are presented throughout the text of this book in italics.

As with all oral histories, the accuracy of Laurie's words cannot be vouched for. Hopefully, in my exposition of his descriptions I have covered anything that is unclear. Should I have made an error here, the fault is entirely mine. The book begins with an historical overview of the manner in which Selby's mercantile trade has depended on the Ouse and the developments that have linked town and river. Laurie's story then follows chronologically as the text covers his family history and tales of his youth, ending with his thoughts in retirement. Sandwiched between that beginning and end of a tale, the core of the book is more thematic, dealing with the growth of the factories in Selby that Laurie's barges serviced, the details of the varying skills required at the Selby and Hull ends of the job and the hazards and challenges of the journey in between. These central chapters call upon Laurie's memories from all parts of his fifty-year career.

In terms of technical matters, in the main weights and measures have been left in the imperial units in which Laurie knew them. When amounts of cargo are referred to, the term 'ton' is used throughout here as the Imperial unit of twenty hundredweight which was the standard when Laurie and his father Sam were trading. The metric unit 'tonne' did not apply until after they ceased work. Lengths are again generally given in feet and inches as that was Laurie's 'lingua franca'. Conversions into metric, where given, are only approximate.

Similarly, modern monetary values have been approximated to give a feel of the worth of a financial transaction, but it is very difficult to convey this accurately, given the need to factor in variables such as the cost of living and variations in the prices of goods. The assumptions of The National Archive's comparison scales have been used throughout to produce the 'modern' values.

A variety of nautical terms that Laurie refers to are defined in the glossary that forms Appendix 3.

A briefer version of Laurie's story was published by Groundwork North Yorkshire in 2011 as part of the 'Hidden Heritage' project, and I must thank them for giving me the opportunity to meet Laurie, and lay the foundations for this project.

I must also thank the following for their assistance in preparation of this volume: the archives of the *Selby Times, York Press* and *Waterways World;* members of Selby Civic Society; members and the archive of Ye Olde Fraternitie of Selebians; Hull History Centre; Hull Maritime Museum; Hull Peoples' Memorial; 'Old Barnsley' at Barnsley Market; Selby and Goole Libraries; Yorkshire Waterways Museum; Susan Butler; Chris Drakes; Michael Pearson; Alice Prince, and members of Laurie's family. My apologies to anyone I have inadvertently missed from this list.

The images in this book are either Laurie's, mine or are appropriately acknowledged in the caption to the photograph. My thanks to all those who have allowed their images to be used. Permission to use an image in this book does not imply that it can be used elsewhere. A few images remain unaccredited, despite efforts to find the appropriate owners of the copyright. If there is a problem in this regard, please contact the publisher.

David Lewis,
Selby, May 2016

Chapter 1

SELBY'S TRADE ON THE YORKSHIRE OUSE

'Selby is situated on the west bank of the Ouse which glides
by in a deep, broad and majestic stream.'
(S.R. Clark's Gazetteer, 1828)

The River Ouse does indeed glide through Selby in a quiet yet stately way, but its passage is now almost completely ignored by those who live in town and style themselves Selebians. There are periodic concerns about flooding and the occasional inconvenience on the rare occasions that the road or rail bridges have to swing open to allow a pleasure boat to pass, but for long periods of time, the river has become an irrelevance.

This worthlessness is a very recent development. From Viking ships coming upriver for the battles of Fulford and Stamford Bridge in 1066 and Abbot Benedict's vision of three swans that led to the foundation of Selby Abbey in 1069, until the final decade of the twentieth century, trade and employment in Selby were centred on the riverside. This chapter describes the history and development of commerce on the river, problems that are encountered in its navigation, and first-hand accounts of those who depended on it for their livelihood.

The Ouse at Selby is no ordinary river. Such is the vastness of the Humber's estuary that the Ouse, one of its two tributaries, experiences tides at Selby, despite being more than sixty miles from the sea. In fact, Selby was not the furthest extent of the tide. Trinity House, the authority on all matters maritime, explained in 1698

'Popleton ffery wch is about 4 miles above ye Citty of York (and) we could not reach yt except upon extraordinary Tides.'

Poppleton is around eighty miles by river from the North Sea. It was only with the construction of Naburn Lock in 1757 that the effects of the tidal flow to York and further up the river were restricted. To gain a full understanding of Selby's river, one needs to begin with a consideration of her tides, meanders and mood swings. A tidal river has many more intriguing properties than one which merely flows in a constant direction at a steady pace. A tide is a mighty pulse of water caused by the gravitational effects of the Sun and Moon. This pulsation of water that brings high tide to the north-east coast of the UK is generated in the Atlantic. A mass of water travels around the northern coast of Scotland and down the eastern one of England, before meeting a similar pulse which has moved up the English Channel. This conflict produces the tidal surge seen as the flood tide that produces a flow that makes it seem that the river is moving uphill.

The actual time of high water on the north-east coast changes the further south one travels. If high water at Aberdeen is at midnight, high water at Whitby is around three in the morning and at Spurn Head 4am. This tide then sweeps into the Humber estuary and high water at Hull will be at around five, at Trent Falls, the confluence of the Ouse and Trent, at 5.30 and at Selby at a little after seven. Poppleton would have been reached around 10am. These periodic changes have a serious effect on river navigation, in three ways, and sailors would have to be aware of the effects of each of them: the length of time the tides 'run'; the change in depth of the river; and the velocity of the current.

This tide does not run for an equal amount of time on all parts of the river. In general, the nearer to the coast, the longer the flood tide holds sway. Because there are two tides every 24½ hours, at the coast, each flood tide runs for just over 6 hours. At Hull the incoming tide runs for about 5½ hours, but at Selby, for only 2½. Like high water, low water occurs at different times on the river. Since the flood tide lasts a shorter time the further you are from the sea, then the duration of the ebb, when water is flowing back towards the sea, must increase to keep the tidal cycle of a high tide every 12¼ hours. So, if the flood at Selby lasts for 2½ hours, after a very short period of slack water the gentler ebb must begin, lasting about 10 hours.

As the tide comes in, water is pushed up the river, so increasing the river's depth. The difference in height between when the river is at its lowest and that when all the flood tide has passed is the river's 'range'. This range depends on the effect of the Moon's gravity on the Earth. Tides are highest at new or full moon, and gradually fall, then rise, in the fortnight between them. In its extreme at Selby the range is 15ft (4.7m). If you are mooring your boat on the river, you need to know how much rope to allow for the tide!

The velocity at which water travels upstream depends on the depth of the channel it meets. As the river becomes shallower, the velocity of the flow increases. On the Ouse at Selby, the flood tide runs at speeds up to 8 knots, which is much faster than most river craft can travel under their own power. The power of the current is not to be treated lightly. The *Gentleman's Magazine* of August 1811 reports that:

'John Bateman of Selby, master of the brig William, was proceeding up the Humber when she was driven by the strength of tide upon Whitton Sand [bank]. The rapidity of the current … forced her broadside [lying across the current] and the captain's wife, two of his children and a female passenger, were drowned as the water rushed into the cabin with overwhelming fury.'

Twice every day, mariners on the Ouse had to get used to these variations in the direction, depth and speed of flow of the river.

A further effect of the tidal flow is a river wave. Under certain conditions, normally around full or new moon, and around the equinoxes in September and March, the incoming rush meets the natural downward flow of the river with such a force that a wave is produced. This effect has long been experienced, and names for it around Yorkshire reflect the language of the Viking invaders of a millennium ago with Norse-based names such as eagre, aegre or aegir.

The wave is more commonly known as a river bore, which is also derived from an Old Norse word, bara, meaning a wave. Whilst the Rivers Severn and Trent are famous for their inland waves, that on the Ouse can be equally spectacular. The bore marks the leading edge of the tide, and once passed, the pulse of water surges upriver at high speed, carrying all manner of flotsam, making an impressive sight for onlookers, and one has to be wary of if it on the river.

The phenomenon moved Elizabethan poet Michael Drayton to write:

'When flood comes to the deep,
The Humber is heard most horribly to roar,
When my aegir comes I make either shore,
Tremble with the sound that I afar do send.'

Francis Drake, historian of York, described the bore in 1736 as 'a strange, back current of water … [it] makes a mighty noise at its approach'. More than a century later, Bulmer's *Gazetteer of the Rivers of the East Riding* in 1892 provides more detail:

'When the tide begins to flow in the [Humber] estuary the waters of the Ouse rise with startling suddenness, and occasionally with considerable violence. This peculiar rising or water-rush is locally known as the "Ager", a name of doubtful origin, but supposed by many writers to have been derived from Oegir, the terrible water-god of our Teutonic ancestors.'

This wave can dislodge vessels at their moorings. A sudden snapping and loosing of the craft into the river results if the bore and its flood tide are not heeded. River workers were aware of its threat and working keel men in Selby would cry 'Wild [or "wor"] aegir' on sighting the crest of the wave.

Construction of river walls at the confluence of Trent and Ouse around 1930 to increase the navigable depth of the river to Goole has reduced the bore's force, but it is still worth looking out for.

Since this flood tide is so powerful, it might be thought that navigation up river would be simple – wait at Hull or Goole until the tide is due, and just surf up on the inrushing 'first of the flood'. Sadly, life isn't that easy. It is certainly the case that ships try to leave their moorings to catch the flood, but the tidal flow actually outruns anything carried on it.

When craft were powered by the wind, the best that could be done was to go with the flood until slack water arrived. Judicious use of sails and tacking across the river could carry a ship a little further upstream, but eventually it would be necessary to drop anchor. Out would come the pack of cards whilst the mariners waited for the tide to turn. Many tides could be needed to bring a sailing ship up from Hull to Selby or York. Instead of lying becalmed, it was possible to tow ships along so-called haling or towing paths. However, like the roads, they could often be so poorly made that they were impossible for horses to use.

The advent of motorised craft in the early part of the nineteenth century overcame these problems to an extent. It was now more possible to keep up with the flow, and a good trip from Hull to Selby could be achieved in six hours.

Working with the tides is not the only problem. The navigable channel of the river constantly varies. Since this channel in the Ouse depends on how the flow of water scours it out, the correct course to follow depends on the time of year and the state of tide. Firstly, particles of mud caught up in the current are responsible for changes in the depth of the navigation channel. The major source of this silt in the river bed derives from the flood tide's work of carrying up mud from the soft cliffs of Holderness. During summer and autumn, the fast-moving flood tide carries material for a considerable distance up-river, but the ebb lacks the power under normal conditions to remove it. On each tide, the bed of the river therefore rises a little. It is only with the

The shifting river channel at a meander

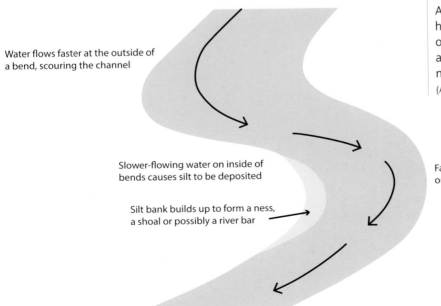

Water flows faster at the outside of a bend, scouring the channel

Slower-flowing water on inside of bends causes silt to be deposited

Silt bank builds up to form a ness, a shoal or possibly a river bar

A diagram showing how the movement of the river current in a meander affects the navigation channel.
(Author)

Fast-flowing water erodes the outer bank of the river

torrents of fresh water caused by winter rain and melting snow that the deposits are washed back out to sea.

A second point to consider is the twistiness of the Ouse's course. Its many hoops and bights, bends and meanders, require careful piloting to keep to the navigable channel, since the depth of water varies across the width of a river bend. Currents in a river tend to flow towards the outside of a bend. Without vigilant steering, craft would go with the flow, giving rise to some problems.

A combination of flow patterns and bends leads to potential problems with grounding. The silt tends to build up in the slacker sections of the river, such as the insides of bends, where nesses form. If your boat was caught on a ness, at the very best, there was a wait of twelve hours for the next high tide. If particularly unfortunate and the level of the tides was dropping from day to day, you might have to wait for a fortnight until the gravity of the moon was at its maximum effect, and the tides were sufficiently high to refloat the vessel. In the meantime, the possibility of the vessel breaking its back by being only partially supported by water was an ever-present problem.

In the slacker water of summer, nesses extend further and further into the river course, leading to shoals of shallow water. If such a shoal develops, in extreme cases river islands can be created, with ebb and flood tides running in different channels around this temporary feature. In the quieter conditions of summer, shoals can stretch across the entire width of the river, creating a bar. These features tend to be washed away when winter rains increase a river's natural flow. Laurie's tales describe how a mariner had to face and surmount these challenges raised by Mother Nature.

A river pilot was skilled indeed to be able to understand and counter all these natural nuances and any craft hoping to voyage successfully to and from Selby and the coast would need to be crewed by seamen astute and experienced enough to deal with such problems. At the very least, boats carried long poles to push the boat away from any shallows and doughty ropes that could be attached to riverside trees to allow muscle power to shift the boat if grounded.

An example of these navigation problems is acutely described by well-known nineteenth century traveller, George Head. He describes the pitfalls involved during his voyage from Selby to Hull that began after breakfast one morning:

'The navigation of the Ouse and Humber, owing to shoals and shifting sands, is as bad as can be, at all times. This morning the tide was fast ebbing, and though starting one minute sooner might possibly have operated in our favour, in point of fact, the chances were about ten to one that we would be stuck in the mud.

'Doubts were soon expressed by those partially acquainted with the river as to whether the ebb was not too far advanced. Before we had been a couple of hours on the way, indications appeared sufficient to set speculation at rest, for the water became as thick as a puddle, so that it actually retarded the rate of the steamer; and two men, one on each side, each with a checkered pole in his hands, continually announced the soundings.

'We were tantalized for some time by hearing "six foot, five foot, five and a half foot, five foot" and so on, till at last came "four and a half foot" and then she stuck.

'As it turned out, this not happening to be the spot whereon the captain had made up his mind to repose, he was active and anxious to get the vessel afloat, and in this object received able support from all his passengers, who, about forty in number, condescendingly acted in concert under his directions, and shuffled across from one side to another so as to keep her going, and prevent her from lying quietly down on the mud.

'Whenever, in a coarse gruff voice, he gave the emphatic word of command "Rowl her," the crowd, like sheep at the bark of a dog, trotted across the deck, treading on one another's heels, and suffering much personal inconvenience. At the same time they hauled upon a rope, previously sent on shore, and made fast to a purchase, till the vessel was disengaged from her soft bed, and again afloat in a channel nearer the shore.

'We proceeded now about two miles farther, when the men with the checkered sounding poles were at work again for a few minutes, and then came an end of all uncertainty, for we touched the ground again, and in a few seconds were laid up in right earnest.

'The captain now was so well prepared for the catastrophe, that not an oar was plied, or the least exertion of any sort made; but here she remained for three hours, during which time an opportunity was afforded to those inclined to reflection to determine the cause why this packet boat might not, by starting some time later, have allowed the people to pass their time at Selby instead of upon this mud bank. On asking eagerly for information on this point, it was hinted that the liquors on board were excellent; but this is mere hearsay.'

Though in medieval times York was an important port, over many years, the Ouse gradually reduced in depth above Selby as summer silting was not overcome by winter floods. Dredging or ploughing the shoals had some effect, but it became ever more difficult for cargo boats to reach York. By 1544, York Corporation noted that its thirty-five-ton sea-going sailing barges were unable to navigate reliably from York to Hull due to lack of depth of water.

On a royal visit to the city in 1617, York Corporation asked London poet Sands Percvine to act the role of the 'Voice of the River', a costumed figure personifying the Ouse, to petition King James I himself on Ouse Bridge. Mr Percvine informed the monarch that his money was urgently required to return the city to her mediaeval glory in the matter of river trade. Sadly, his role did not bring the relief requested.

By the late seventeenth century, it was feared that unless something were done, the laden ships and barges of the time would only be able to reach the city twice a month, on the biggest or spring tides at times of full moon and new moon. Surveyor Thomas Surbey was asked in 1699 to find a way of restoring the tide to York. The commonly held idea was to cut across all the bends in the river below Selby. At a cost of £40,000 (perhaps £4 million in modern terms), river flow would increase and so reduce silting. However, Surbey was able to demonstrate that the additional flow of tide gained by this expensive solution would only give York four inches more water on the highest of tides, and so this expenditure would not be a good investment.

His advice instead was that 'wee conceive a Lock to be ye best and cheapest way of Improvement of yo'r Navigation and trade' and that York should build a river lock at Naburn, to ensure water levels to York remained at a navigable depth. His estimate of the cost of this lock was £5,500 (£430,000), around an eighth of the cost of cutting the corners, and much more effective. However, York Corporation was not convinced, and despite thanking Surbey and paying him £25 (£2,000) for his services, almost sixty years would elapse before the lock was finally built and opened in 1757.

Although the weir at Naburn now guaranteed a good depth of water at York, trade to York was waning, as the sheer distance of the haul up river, almost eighty miles, was too time-consuming. Selby's advantage was its intermediate position between York and Hull, closer to the coast and without the need to navigate yet more bends and shoals between it and York.

Even before York's problems with river silting, Selby had had a valuable river trade. In 1204, its annual value was £263 (£150,000), placing the town twenty-fourth of thirty-five trading towns, behind Hull with £5,170 and York with £2,631, but putting Whitby's £3 yearly return to shame! There is some evidence that trade was international, as a merchant referred to as Alan the Frenchman held much property in Selby's riverside street, Ousegate, at this time, and a century later, two wine merchants from Gascony are recorded as being active in the town. In 1339, Edward III allowed reloading of goods at Selby without payment of further customs dues, which meant that Selby was a source of a sufficient volume of goods bound for the continent to make this worthwhile.

The major moving force for medieval trade in Selby was the Abbey. Selby Abbey's walls encompassed the current Market Place, and goods flowed between the Market Place around the Abbey and Micklegate to riverside wharves and jetties. The monastery and merchants worked in tandem, with the result that Selby became the hub of local, regional and national trade. Contemporary records show that lead, timber and stone for the Abbey passed from the river to the Abbey, along with materials for wider trade such as copper and iron, cloth and coal, oils, spices and leather.

The river was a much more efficient artery of transport than the roads. As Farley states:

'when roads were the merest tracks … the river afforded an easy thoroughfare for goods and chattels carried on rafts and coracles.'

River-based activities also implied shipbuilding. John the Shipwright is recorded in Ousegate in the fourteenth century, and

Selby's reputation for quality shipbuilding stretches back centuries as Henry V's ship *Catherine*, involved in transport to Agincourt, was built at an Ousegate yard. Life along Ousegate was probably boisterous and court rolls record instances of small-scale illegalities and people-trafficking that would not seem out of place today. For instance, in 1472 John Coke was accused of running a 'nocturnal gambling centre' whilst Robert Browne was charged with 'harbouring Scots and other suspect people'.

In general, the medieval picture is of a thriving port for transhipment of goods and small scale boat manufacture, which continued until the late seventeenth century. Typical cargoes listed in 1698 include coal (from Newcastle!) hay, corn, wool, lead, butter, rape seed and tallow. Shipbuilding and allied activities no doubt continued along Ousegate. A map of 1790 shows 'Mr. Sheppard's shipyard' just next to the mouth of the newly-built Selby Canal. A few years after Sheppard's yard is recorded, John Foster appears on the scene, firstly in 1804 as sole owner of a 144ton brig, *Cromwell Bottom*, and in 1805 of an 81ton sloop, *Britannia*. In 1807, he is reported as both a shipbuilder and owner:

'Launched from the shipyard of Mr John Foster, Selby, a fine new ship called the *Seaton*, upwards of 300 tons burthen. The launch was remarkably good, attended by a great concourse of people, and the hilarity of the day was kept up by Mr Foster, the builder, and principal owner, giving an elegant dinner to a party of select friends, and distributing plenty of punch and ale to some hundreds of his workmen and attendants.'

The shipyard then went into the hands of Samuel Gutteridge, who ran a successful business for many years. His shipyard not only had a dry dock, but also sufficient capacity for launching four large ships. *The Northern Star* of 29 February 1840 reported:

'This noble art of shipbuilding is now in greater activity at Selby, Mr Gutteridge having commissions of several large brigs and schooners. There are in his yard three ships on the stocks at present.'

The growing importance of Goole meant that shipbuilding in Selby went into decline in the 1850s. Thomas Green took over from Gutteridge in 1856, followed in short order by James Banks, then Joseph Burton. More long-standing names then came to the fore with Henry Connell setting up a yard that lasted until the 1950s, with Cochrane's neighbouring yard remaining in business until the 1990s.

Laurie's working life involved him with both Connell's and Cochrane's shipyards. Mountain's *History of Selby* reported that over 800 coasters were dealt with annually at the wharves on the Ouse in 1800 with around 370,000 tons of goods passing through what was effectively a major inland port. Trade continued to slowly improve, and twenty years later, in the summer quarter of 1819 alone, figures from the *Yorkshire Gazette* show almost 500 ships used the port of Selby. That equates to around seven vessels per working day. These vessels came from all parts of the English coast ranging from Sussex to Northumberland. Not only goods, but passengers were also carried, and as the nineteenth century advanced, these sailings became more regular. In 1814, the steamboat *Caledonia* journeyed between Hull and Selby. By 1822, a steam packet service existed between Hull and London, and three years later a weekly service linked Selby and Yarmouth, with occasional voyages to Rotterdam.

In 1828, a Customs House was erected on Ousegate, to allow goods to pass through Goole or Hull without needing to wait for inspection onboard. In the 1840s, the *Penny Magazine* reported:

'There is a branch custom-house at Selby, so that vessels can proceed direct to any part of the kingdom. About 1,000 ships with cargoes clear coastwise annually.'

Another passenger vessel was the *Joanna*, which left 'for Hull and all places adjoining the Rivers Ouse and Humber' every Monday. The return journey was advertised for Thursdays 'if wind and weather permit' implying that they might not always do this. The possible problems of the journey have already been seen in George Head's item. The single fare on the *Joanna* was 2/- (£3) and food was available for an extra 6d (80p) for men but merely 4d (55p) for women. Around 20,000 passengers annually were using the steam packet service to Hull by 1830, with the encouragement of Selby entrepreneurs including James Audus.

Samuel Lewis reports in 1831 that:

'The chief article exported is stone, which is sent coastwise: ships of one hundred and fifty to two hundred tons' burden navigate to Selby; steam-boats pass daily to and from Hull, and there are daily communications with London, and every port on the coast: here is a ship-yard, in which vessels of considerable burden are built.'

Selby was once again a thriving commercial hub.

The next stage of Selby's commercial development presaged the decline of river trade. Lewis records that:

'It is in contemplation to construct a railway from Selby to Leeds, which, if effected, will materially promote the trading interests of the town.'

The railway opened in 1834, but as Selby was the terminus of the line from Leeds, river carriage onwards to Hull remained highly popular. New, steam-powered vessels had greatly reduced the dependence on wind and tidal conditions, and despite the shoals and shallows, new ships were built for the journey between Selby and Hull, using the modern technology of iron instead of wood. The *Leeds Mercury* of 30 January 1835 tells us:

'The bold and successful experiment of constructing vessels of iron seems destined to come into extensive operation … iron vessels only draw 2'6' (0.7m) not the 4' 0' (1.2m) for wood'.

A later issue of the paper, on 7 March 1835 described yet another new launch:

'Iron Steam Packet "Railway"'. On Thursday last a large and beautiful steam packet, constructed entirely of iron, was launched from the yard of Mr Gutteridge, shipbuilder, Selby. She received the name of *Railway* and is intended to ply between the depot of the Leeds and Selby Railway at Selby, and Hull and to carry passengers only. She is so constructed as to draw the least possible draught of water and it is full expected she will be able to make the passage at all times of the tide without grounding. The *Railway* is the property of James Audas [sic], Esq. of Selby and is commanded by Mr Camsell, an experienced Captain in the London and Selby coasting trade.'

Selby's river-based commerce was booming. High quality warehouses were put up along Ousegate to reflect the opulence of the times, with superior residences for ship's officers and shipping agents being constructed in town. The rail and river combination became widely popular. The *Leeds Mercury* reported in 1836 that it was 'now possible to travel from London to Hull in under a day'. Excursions were arranged to make use of the link, but only for a few years until the railway line was extended to Hull in 1840.

Cargoes now reflected the agricultural area around Selby with loads to and from the mills for flour, seeds and animal feedstuffs. At this time, control of the waterway from York to Goole was with York Corporation, which provided a public towing service. The wharf below the railway bridge was called the Corporation Wharf to show this.

Coal supplies from the West Riding came via the Selby Canal and thence upriver behind Corporation tugs until 1947. Rowntree's chocolate factory at York was another customer,

A busy scene at York Corporation Wharf, Selby in the latter part of the nineteenth century. (Richard Moody)

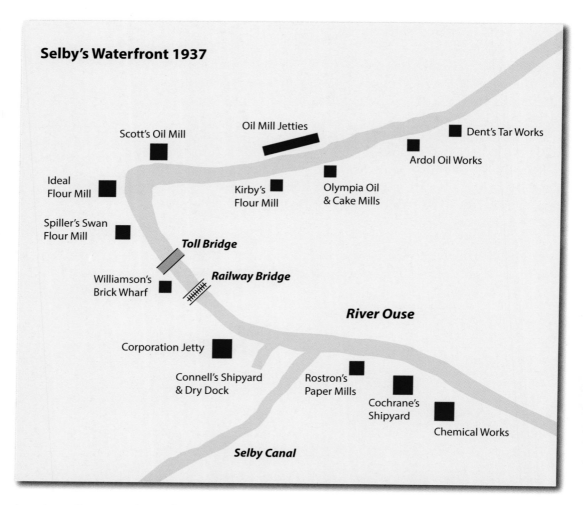

Selby's Waterfront 1937

Scott's Oil Mill

Oil Mill Jetties

Dent's Tar Works

Ardol Oil Works

Ideal
Flour Mill

Kirby's
Flour Mill

Olympia Oil
& Cake Mills

Spiller's Swan
Flour Mill

Toll Bridge

Williamson's
Brick Wharf

Railway Bridge

River Ouse

Corporation Jetty

Connell's Shipyard
& Dry Dock

Rostron's
Paper Mills

Cochrane's
Shipyard

Chemical Works

Selby Canal

Locations of
waterfront industries
in Selby in 1937.
(Alice Prince)

with several vessels a week travelling up the Ouse and Foss. Messrs Leetham's, whose mill was in a fine riverside building off Walmgate in York was also a customer for large loads of grain and seeds for milling. In the Selby area, on the bend of the river above the toll bridge, Swan's ideal flour mill of 1935 received grain. Around Scott's Bight, what was first known as 'OCO' (Olympia Cake and Oil) and latterly as BOCM (British Oil and Cake Mills) opened at Barlby, circa 1910. The name derives from the two staple parts of the business. The mill crushed seed to extract oil, and the compressed material remaining turned into 'cake' for cattle. OCO/BOCM were the Dews' family's main employers. In the years between the two world wars, Selby's waterfront was teeming with industry as the diagram shows.

In the years after the Second World War, there was another boom in trade on the Ouse in Selby. Towing dumb barges still had a part to play. According to Laurie:

'River traffic was very busy … OCO had to engage as many tugs as they could to haul barges to and from Selby. Each barge could hold 225 tons loaded to the scuppers.'

These tugs were not only company owned, but also hired in from municipal operators such as York Corporation and Goole Towing Company and individuals such as Peter Foster and Wilf Akester. Trade improved further when BOCM had a series of motorised barges built at Dunston's of Thorne during the 1950s that would hold 250 tons or so. Larger 'coasters' came up river to Selby. These were ships that carried loads in the region of 500-1,000 tons around the coast of the UK or on cross-channel routes. The loads were of a similar order to those that could be carried on a group of four dumb barges, but using coasters meant that there was no need for transfer between boat and barge in Hull, thus saving time and money. By 1966, around 200 coasters per year were berthing at Selby. The ready availability of docking space along Ousegate and wide transport links allowed goods to be transferred swiftly in Selby for onward distribution. There were both private haulage contractors and rail sidings linked to the national network. Around 600,000 tonnes of bulk traffic was being moved through Selby in the 1960s, with much of it linked to Rotterdam.

Even the replacement of the old road toll bridge took into account the blossoming river trade. The *Selby Times* reported in 1969:

'Longer spans mean greater openings for more coasters, the journeys of which are increasing monthly.'

One example of a bulk load was molasses for Sturge Chemicals in Denison Road. Jim Wildash, a chemist in the labs at Sturge in the 1970s, recalled how the product used to arrive:

'We used to ship molasses in from Europe and bring in 1,000 tonnes by ship up the Ouse and used the jetty at Cochrane's shipyard. We put a pipe in from the factory to the shipyard and of course these things arrived at very awkward times 'cause you had to rely on the tide and a 1,000 tonne ship was one of the largest that you could get up the Ouse.

'It used to take nearly all night to offload the cargo, and by the next morning we were down to the last amounts in the bottom of each tank and I had to actually go and look in each tank to make sure that all the molasses was out.

'And then of course when they went you had to let go of the ropes before they went. I can remember on one occasion to get back down to Hull and out into the North Sea they had to turn the boat. If they turned it too early the bow would stick into the other side of the bank and on one occasion he actually got stuck across the river. His bow was in one bank and his stern was breached in our side of the bank and he had to wait until the tide came up before it could get away. It was a couple of hours there.'

Other bulk loads included coal tar from York gasworks, creosote, coal for domestic and industrial use, newsprint for the Evening Press, and seeds and rice for the mills. Some return cargoes were available, mainly animal cake. Unloading operations in Selby were mostly carried out by locally-owned firms using mainly non-unionised labour. This led to problems in the disputes and transport strikes in the 1970s and 1980s. In the early 1970s there was unrest in the docks, as registered dockers fought to maintain their long-standing methods of unloading goods by hoist and crane as opposed to new ways of handling goods as the metal storage containers that are so common today began to be introduced. Whilst the power of the unions was such that an official strike could close a port like Hull, there were several 'unregistered' or so-called 'pirate' ports such as Selby where owners could request their ships unload.

Oughtred and Harrison, owners of the major wharf in Selby, said in June 1972, with a degree of trepidation, 'As far as we know, the pickets are coming any day now … we have no plans for what to do when they arrive.'

Graeme Pickering, manager at Viking Shipping in Ousegate, whose company was one of the last to use the Ouse-side wharves, described how he saw the industrial unrest:

'… in the 70s and certainly before the docks in Goole and Hull, Immingham got their act together, when the dockers used to rule that it was an official strike … [Hull was closed but] … Selby was now private owned so they never went on strike.'

With union solidarity, it wasn't just dock strikes that could cause disruption; sympathetic action from other unions could cause unrest too. An example was the miners' strikes of 1974. Graeme explained:

'… in the coal strike from the 70s, obviously all the flying pickets would come down here so you'd have a complete road full of tipper lorries … and you'd have all the flying pickets as well. It was good natured but it never stopped us working 'cause our men sometimes weren't in a union, rightly or wrongly. If they weren't in a union obviously we came and worked so vessels that were supposed to go to Goole or Immingham or Hull, if they were small enough they'd come up here to get discharged.'

Yet some people remained confident. Dennis Wheatley, then General Manager of Selby Wharf was in upbeat mood in November 1983 when the biggest ever single cargo unloaded in Selby, 1,555 tons of sheanuts from the Ivory Coast for use in bakery and confectionery, was delivered:

'Trade is booming. Inland ports are coming into their own because water transport is so much cheaper than road'.

But containerisation swept away not only long established methods of unloading cargoes, but also how such cargoes were dealt with. As soon as the ubiquitous 32-ton container lorry began to ply its trade on roll-on, roll-off ferries, everything changed. Huge cargo ships with thousands of containers meant that goods could move in a single container from supplier direct to port then directly to customer. There was no longer a need for expensive and time-consuming transhipment. The final type of trading vessels that have serviced Westmill Foods were the so-called 'LASH' barges. Originally beginning on the Humber for a couple of years from 1974, and returning to the Ouse in 1997, these huge boxes (60x30ft) were an attempt to adapt the containerisation idea to an entirely aquatic mode. Each water–borne container can carry ten times the load of a lorry, 380 tons. Huge 'mother ships' carry around 100 of these monster boxes across the oceans, and berth in modern mega-ports like Immingham, giving the economies of scale. Tugs then pilot the containers upriver in pairs.

Despite such a method of delivery bringing over 600 tons of rice at a time to the mill without the use of a coaster, the operation was not profitable and ended in the early years of the current century. With this failure, there is effectively no regular commercial trade on the Ouse, bringing to an end almost 800 years of recorded goods conveyance by river. The Ousegate wharves below the Road Bridge still stand, but are clearly incapable of receiving any shipping as they are redeveloped for housing. The fine Victorian frontages of the warehouses and properties along the length of the street that still survive reflect the centuries of prosperity but also exhibit the sad grandeur of emptiness and decay. This is all a far cry from the days only a generation or so ago when coasters cruised up to Selby on the flood tide, and the pubs of Ousegate resounded to Dutch, German and other European tongues. In the public bars, merchant seamen whiled away the time whilst their ships were unloaded, playing cards and waiting for the tide to turn to allow their return to the open sea.

These sailors impatiently awaited the ebb tide. Sadly, Selby's maritime trade has not received its ebb with such eagerness; there is no prospect of a flood of new business to revive the commerce.

Chapter 2

SOAPY JOE COMES TO SELBY

Laurie's father and grandfather, Sam and Bill Dews, were watermen through and through. The transformation of Sam and Bill from being jobbing bargemen to being part of a dedicated team working the Ouse between Hull and Selby is down to the economic expansion of Joseph Watson and Sons – known to all as 'Soapy Joe' – from Leeds to Selby. One of Bill and Sam's regular jobs was to run to Joe Watson's soap mill on the River Aire at Leeds. Watson's enterprise had grown from modest beginnings in his grandfather's tannery business in 1816 near the family's farm in Horsforth, to the north-west of Leeds into a major manufacturing business. Soapy Joe's was based at the Whitehall Road, Leeds, by the River Aire. Vegetable oils such as palm oil from crushing palm kernels in works in Hull were delivered by barge along the River Aire to be processed into products such as Matchless Cleanser, Venus Soap and Nubolic Detergent Soap. Watson's works was one of the largest soap factories in the country, employing over 700 people in the late nineteenth century, making over 600 tons of soap a week.

He was hugely enterprising and encouraged sales of his products by national competitions such as the one illustrated below from the *Illustrated London News* of 31 December 1898, where by saving and then sending off soap wrappers, customers could enter a draw for highly valuable prizes. In 1900, an average annual wage for a labourer was around £60, so the thought of winning £100 just for sending in some soap wrappers was quite a draw. The fact that Watson could give away almost £1,750 per month – worth perhaps £100,000 today – also gives an idea of how much profit there was in the cleaning trade.

Although production of these brands ceased many years ago, the names remain relatively well-known from their appearance on heritage-styled enamel advertising signs.

LEFT: Enamelled advert for Watson's 'Matchless Cleaner', one of his most popular products.

RIGHT: Advert for Watson's Prize Draw from the *Illustrated London News*, 31 December 1898.

(Author's collection)

Watson was not merely interested in soap. His company also imported resin and tallow, made glycerine for dynamite manufacture, and dealt in hides and skins. The oils extracted in Leeds to make soap could also be used in the margarine and paint businesses. The by-product of the oil's extraction could be used as animal feed, firing Watson's interests in modernizing agricultural practices. During the first decade of the twentieth century, Watson was in competition in the soap and cleansing business with William Lever of Lever Brothers and Port Sunlight fame. After an unsuccessful attempt to merge the businesses to create a monopoly in 1906, over the course of the next decade Lever Brothers effectively took control of Watson's company. However, the founding and development of Watson's factory in Selby preceded that final loss of influence.

Watson's factory was on the River Aire in Leeds. The difficulties of navigation into Leeds via the River Aire convinced Watson that he needed a new factory, with easier access for the delivery of raw materials, and independent of the seed-crushing mills in Hull, to maximize his profits. A greenfield site near to a navigable river was needed. Constructing a factory at Barlby, just north of Selby on the River Ouse, with good rail connections, and on the major road network as well was the ideal place. The fact that Selby had an available work force, was at the heart of an agricultural area with a ready market for animal feed products, and had land to allow him to indulge his plans in the agricultural sphere were bonuses.

Watson founded the Olympia Agricultural Co. Ltd in 1909. To feed the mills, all that was needed now was to engage a reliable company of bargemen to bring the seed up the Ouse from Hull to the new mills. This was the link between the Dews' family fortunes and those of Soapy Joe's.

Laurie describes the approach that Watson made to his granddad Bill:

'He said, "Why don't you come and work for me and I'll build you a boat that will carry 200 tons. I will provide you with all the tackle and we will work by thirds. One third for me and two thirds for you and you won't have to keep pumping her bilges and giving her a bucket of sawdust and ashes to stop her leaking."'

As described in chapter 5, Bill Dews had been skipper of the keel *Ada Dews*, named after his wife, since the 1890s. The *Ada Dews* was a handsome vessel, but by 1909, she (the ship, not his wife!) was showing her age. The prospect of a new craft and guaranteed work was very tempting, and Bill agreed to the deal. The seed-crushing machines of Olympia Oil and Cake Company, or OCO, began the next year.

'So Granddad Bill sold the *Ada Dews* and went to work for Soapy Joe and Dad went mate with him. The first ship, the Leeds Comet, was built by Henry Scarr at Howden Dyke in 1910. Many old keelmen followed suit, selling their keels and going to work for Joe Watson. All his barges were named after heavenly objects like Comet, Venus and Orbit [there is a full list in Appendix 1]. Ships were built to last in those days. The Comet was still working 70 years later under the ownership of Wilf Akester, and was not finally broken up until 1994 at Viking in Goole.'

Watson's OCO factory on Barlby Road Selby in the second decade of the twentieth century.
(Susan Butler /Howdenshire History)

This philanthropic act on Watson's behalf engendered tremendous loyalty in his barge crews, which produced dividends in later years.

'When times were hard in the Depression in the late 1920s and early 1930s, the firm continued to employ the captains who were paid by thirds, just like in Joe Watson's day.'

But, out of his money, the captain had to employ a mate. However, the company only paid the captain if there was a cargo to move, so no cargo, no pay! If there was no cargo to move, the firm tied the barges up in the Queen's Dock in Hull.

'Even though they didn't get any pay, they felt they were still responsible for the barges that Joe Watson had given them, so the old barge skippers kept going down to the docks to check up on their craft.'

Initially, the mills dealt with linseed, cottonseed and soya beans. By 1913 the plant could deal with palm kernels, copra and groundnuts. Around 3,000 tons of seed were dealt with weekly as the factory worked continually from 6a.m. Monday to noon on Saturday. Whilst seed to be crushed was the main cargo that the OCO barges carried, other, liquid cargoes were also sometimes transported. These liquids included molasses and palm oil. Carrying bulk liquid cargoes was potentially more hazardous than carrying solid ones, as the rocking action of a tide on the river could set up a similar motion in the cargo. If there was no bulkhead running the length of the hold, such a swaying liquid could eventually cause a barge to 'lay over' and eventually capsize. Such capsizings could be both dangerous and comical.

'In the 1930s, the rolling of a cargo of 150 tons of palm oil on the Selby Castor *caused the barge to become stuck across Selby Toll Bridge. The current in the river set the oil oscillating and the crew knew she was going to sink. The mate, Josh Ward, clambered up the wooden buttress of the bridge, but skipper Andy Wray went overboard, fortunately to be rescued from the river near to the railway bridge.'*

There's no comedy in that, but what was amusing was the Selby townsfolk's reaction to the sinking. The weather was quite cold, so as the palm oil rose from the sunken barge, it solidified and floated on the surface of the Ouse. Selebians, being canny Yorkshire types scooped up the oil in bags and took it to market to sell! The cargoes of seed and nuts came from freighters that docked in Hull, so at the very least, fifteen full barges needed to discharge at Barlby every week to keep the factory running at full capacity. Watson's fleet eventually numbered thirty-four barges, meaning that each barge had to make a delivery at least once a fortnight.

Watson's OCO produced oil that could be used in the manufacture of margarine and paint, and from the remaining compressed husks, animal feeds for dairy cows, calves, lambs and pigs could be made. By 1915, this seed-crushing and oil-extracting business had become the largest of its kind in Europe. Once the seed has been crushed to extract the oil, the solid material left is a valuable animal feed. This product was not only sold locally but could also be a useful load for the barges to take back down to Hull. This was the 'Cake' part of the OCO.

Later in the decade, Watson over-reached himself financially and had to sell OCO to the Dutch firm Jurgens.

Whilst the ultimate successors to Watson's firm, in the shape of 'ForFarmers', still have a presence at Barlby, little of Watson's factory remains. For the remainder of the text, 'OCO' and

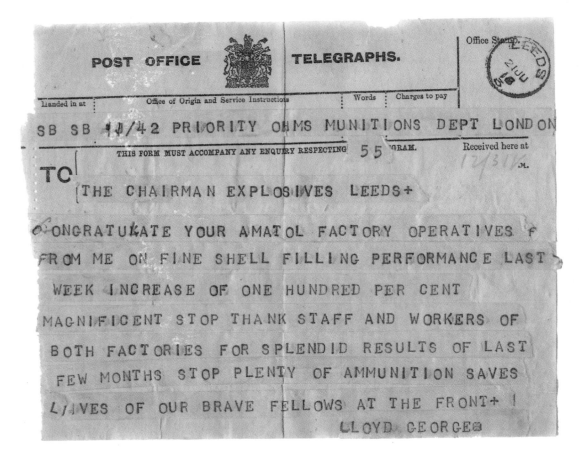

POST OFFICE		TELEGRAPHS.	Office Stamp

Handed in at	Office of Origin and Service Instructions	Words	Charges to pay

SB SB 11/42 PRIORITY OHMS MUNITIONS DEPT LONDON

THIS FORM MUST ACCOMPANY ANY ENQUIRY RESPECTING 55 GRAM.   Received here at

TO

[THE CHAIRMAN EXPLOSIVES LEEDS+

CONGRATULATE YOUR AMATOL FACTORY OPERATIVES
FROM ME ON FINE SHELL FILLING PERFORMANCE LAST
WEEK INCREASE OF ONE HUNDRED PER CENT
MAGNIFICENT STOP THANK STAFF AND WORKERS OF
BOTH FACTORIES FOR SPLENDID RESULTS OF LAST
FEW MONTHS STOP PLENTY OF AMMUNITION SAVES
LIIVES OF OUR BRAVE FELLOWS AT THE FRONT+
          LLOYD GEORGE

Congratulatory telegram to Watson from then Prime Minister Lloyd George.

'BOCM' refer to the seed crushing mills at Barlby, between 1910 and 1990. A further name linked to OCO is Ardol. This part of the factory was involved in chemically hardening whale or fish oil into fats without the unpleasant odour that would taint soap. The name presumably is a shortening of hard or hardening oil. This only lasted until 1920, although the name did resurface as one of OCO's tugs.

Watson built a 'model village' of around 350 houses for his workers at Barlby, in an echo of Cadbury at Bournville and Rowntree at New Earswick, but Watson also included a licensed premises, the Olympia Hotel, as part of the provision, along with ten acres of recreation fields and nine acres of allotments. The entire operation employed up to 1,000 workers. The factory area was around 50 acres, with a further 100 acres or so given over to the firm's farming subsidiary, and a further 900 acres let out to farmers on a third-party basis.

Watson was also involved in the munitions trade in the First World War. The factory at Barlby was involved in the production of poisonous phosgene, and Watson was also party to the setting up of a large munitions factory at Barnbow to the east of Leeds, and received a telegram from the Prime Minister, Lloyd George, thanking him for his contribution to the war effort.

A final OCO subsidiary was Selby Warehousing and Transport (or SW&T), which owned parts of the business for legal reasons. It ceased to function in the 1940s, but is mentioned by Laurie in his songs in Appendix 2. After the war, Watson continued his philanthropic ventures, donating £50,000 to the Leeds General Infirmary in 1921. He was created Baron Manton in 1922, but died of a heart attack whilst riding out to hunt before he could take up residence at his newly acquired estate in Warwickshire.

Although much of the BOCM works closed in the 1990s, the factory buildings at Barlby remained intact until the early part of this century. The Barnbow factory became Vickers, and, whilst now disused, the site can still be seen from the railway line to the east of Leeds on the journey from Selby. The bulk silos on Barlby Road were only demolished in 2008, with the majority of the factory buildings following in the next couple of years. The allotments are still tilled and the Recreation Ground where local Olympic athlete Stanley Englehart trained for the 1932 Games is still in place. However, there are plans for a large housing and light business development on the site. Whilst it is good that a derelict site is brought back into profitable use, such a development will wipe away many traces of what was one of the largest and most important industrial enterprises in the north of England.

Chapter 3

A BARGEMAN'S LIFE ON THE OUSE IN THE 1920s

Laurie's parents, Elisabeth and Sam Dews. (Laurie Dews)

After the First World War, Granddad Bill went skipper of the *Leeds Eclipse*, one of Watson's dumb barges, but Sam became skipper of the first dual purpose oil and solids-carrying barge, the *Selby Vega*. All of Watson's dumb barges had celestial names; a full list is given in Appendix 1. Laurie still has Sam's work log from 1919–1934, a fifty-page volume documenting Sam's day-to-day experiences and serves well to show the kind of working conditions an Ouse bargeman endured in the 1920s.

Sam's log starts in earnest in 1920, by which time the effects of the First World War had subsided to some extent, and so to a degree, working conditions had returned to 'normal'. The factory at Barlby was getting back towards full production. Consideration of one of Sam's round trips on the *Selby Vega* gives an idea of what a bargeman's work involved. This page of the log book, and in particular the trip starting on 18 March is a good example of such a round trip. Sam got paid every time the boat completed a round trip to Hull and back. By comparing the dates when he got paid, you can see that the average round trip took about ten days. No two

2 3.20	Settled up some money	2 9 5		
8	Discharged and towed to Hull Alex. dock			
10	Settled up freight 133 bombay 29 PK	201 10	2 10 0
11	Towed out of Alex. dock to Albert dock tug Rover			
12	Started loading PK out of wagons in E R warehouse			
13	finished loading 172 tons			
14	towed to Selby tug Lity			
15	Discharged P K			
16	Towed to Hull tug Robie			
18	Started loading ground nuts in shells ss Hustienes settled up P K	11 12 4	2 10 0
19	finished loading			
22	left Hull tug midge landed Blacktoft fog arrived Selby night tide and started discharging			
23	finished discharging and got the anchor on board which was lost at the bridge			
24	towed to Hull Albert dock			
25	Started loading PK	12 6 3	2 10 0
26	settled up freight			
27	finished loading 175 tons PK			
29	Towed to Selby tug Robie			
30	Discharged P K			
31	Started loading oil in drums			
1.4.20	finished loading 250 " 181 tons			
3	Towed to Hull tug Robie			
6	settled up P K freight 155 tons	120 7	2 10 0
8	Started Discharging ss Rosyth			
17	finished discharging '' Rosyth and settled up freight	15 12 11	
19	towed out of Humber dock to hab			
22	Started loading beans Allantic Wav			
24	finished			
26	towed to Selby tug Robie			
27	Discharged beans			
28	towed to Hull tug Robie Harbour			
29	settled up freight beans 200 tons	12 16 4	2 10 0
30	Started loading bombay Gar. ware			
4.5	finished loading			
5	towed to Selby tug Robie and started discharging			

Extract from Sam Dews' log, 1920. (Laurie Dews)

trips are the same – different ships, different cargoes, different tugs and a different set of conditions on each occasion.

So, what happened on the trip that began on Thursday, 18 March? Sam went to the Shipping Agent's office to pick up his payment for the previous load of 172 tons of 'PK' or Pine Kernels. As the barge could hold 200 tons, the vessel had been comfortably, but not dangerously, full. He got paid £11/12/4d, or in decimal terms, £11.62, a return of about 1/5d or 7p per ton.

This can be estimated at around £300 and £1.75 per ton in 2016 values. Out of this the mate has to be paid his £2/10/- (£2.50, £75 today). Having picked up his money, Sam was directed to his next job, loading groundnuts in their shells, from the SS *Hurliness*. The *Hurliness* was typical of the boats that the barge trade served. It was a 3,000-tonner, built in 1899 and belonged to the Reardon Smith line, who were involved in the coal trade to South America, from where these ground nuts may have been sourced as a return cargo. Fortunately, the *Hurliness* seems to have been berthed close to the Vega. Were she not to have been, then Sam and his mate would have either needed a tug to be taken to the appropriate dock, or had to use sheer muscle power to manoeuvre the barge across the dock using warping line and boat hook.

It took at least a day to load, but the barge finally was full of cargo. Unusually, the tonnage is not recorded, but by comparison with money received from other cargoes on the same page, it must have been close to the limit of 200 tons. Before Sam could consider the job done, he had to secure his load. Pine kernels had to be kept dry, so Sam would have to make sure that his hatch covers were securely on to stop any rain coming in, and that they were secured against any movement by hammering the battin' irons in. In other words, Sam had to batten down the hatches. Sam also had to position his barge to allow for rapid exit onto the river when tide time came along. Tide time was about an hour after the flood had passed the docks, and it made sense for the tug and its barges to catch the tide. But there were usually four barges linked to an OCO tug, and there were many barges in the lock waiting to be tugged to many other destinations apart from Selby. So, before Sam could rest, he had to moor up close to the other Selby barges,

Blacktoft Jetty
in 1947.

(Susan Butler/
Howdenshire History)

expending more muscle power on boathook and warping line, ready to rope up to the tug in time for tide time.

As it was a weekend, we must presume that the barge was moored up in the docks for two days awaiting a tug. Bargemen didn't always have the weekend off. It was very much a matter of fitting in with the shifts of the dockers, the availability of a tug and the state of the tide, but generally speaking, bargemen were keen to get their cargo moved and unloaded, as the sooner they did that, the sooner they got paid. Looking at the previous weekend, it can be seen that the days were taken up with loading and being tugged up to Selby.

On Monday 22, the tug *Midge* – a veteran built in 1861 – took on the tow. Laurie refers to the tug *Robie* as being the main player in moving the dumb barges between Hull and Selby, but from studying the extracts of Sam's log, it becomes clear that the OCO barges were pulled by many vessels. The *Midge* was, at the time, owned by Charles Kent of Hull, so presumably was hired by OCO for this trip. The weather conditions weren't favourable, so the convoy had to take refuge at Blacktoft Jetty, about half way between Hull and Selby. The jetty here is substantial and a well-known 'refuge' for ships if weather conditions were poor or the water level was falling. There was also a pub handy!

As Sam describes arriving in Selby on the night tide, the barges must have waited a good few hours at Blacktoft, as there is an approximately twelve-hour gap between flood tides. Although it must have been a long day, unloading began straight away, and was complete by the Tuesday. Since the boats came up on the night tide, and it was March, presumably it was dark when the *Vega* passed through Selby's bridges. Passage of Selby's bridges called for smart navigation, sometimes using the anchor as a drag to aid steering. In this case there must have been a mishap, as, after unloading, Sam picked up an anchor from the bridge men.

Once unloaded and fully-equipped, the *Vega* would be tied up at one of Selby's jetties to await a tug back down river. This happened on Wednesday, travelling empty to Albert Dock, to begin loading with pine kernels, before getting paid £12/6/3d for the groundnut cargo on Friday, 26 March.

So, a 'normal round' of nine days, including two days enforced rest, the dangers of fog, working all hours to unload, losing an anchor and a tow back empty brought in just £350 at today's values.

Throughout the previous year Sam recorded the weight of each cargo carried and how much he got paid for that transport. By tallying that data, it can be seen that from February 1919, when the log begins, until the end of the year, the *Vega* carried 2,577 tons of cargo, mainly of different vegetable products that OCO could crush for oil. These included: linseed, also supplied to crushing mills in Gainsborough, Beverley and Hull; ground nuts; palm kernels; 'beans', probably soya beans; copra, the dried flesh of the coconut; black seed; Bombay seed; cotton seed, which could be both black or white so Sam's reference to 'black seed' is presumably black cotton.

Bombay and cotton seeds are effectively both seeds of the cotton plant and black seed could be an Asian seed from a plant belonging to the buttercup family, or just black cotton.

Sam was paid £255/12/11d (£255.65 or about £7,000 in 2016 values) for carrying that cargo. That's an average rate of almost 2/- (10p, £2.75 in 2016 value) per ton. Later in the decade, the rate of pay was gradually reduced, in line with the recession and depression of the later 1920s.

A second extract takes us forward a year to 1921. At the top of the page, Sam is still running the *Vega*, but on 7 July he took charge – without any ceremony noted in the log – of his new boat, *Selby Taurus* which served the Dews family for much of the next thirty years. The *Taurus* was built at Thorne rather than Beverley, and carried solely dry goods rather than the dual capabilities of the *Vega*. A full list of construction details is given in Appendix 1.

A decade earlier, Soapy Joe had promised Bill that he would supply everything that was needed on the *Leeds Comet*. We don't have that inventory, but Laurie does still have the original inventory for Great Uncle Abe's *Selby Virgo*. Sam would have had to check and sign that everything on this comprehensive list was present, correct and shipshape, and was responsible for keeping it that way. Items would be replaced for free if they suffered fair wear and tear, but if something was broken, lost overboard or stolen – all of which happened on the *Taurus* in the next fifteen years – the replacement cost came from the skipper's pocket.

Most of the equipment is obvious, but there were some more obscure but vital items on the list.

- A marlinspike is a device used to help the bargemen splice pieces of rope or wire together.
- A stower (pronounced stour) is a long oar/boathook used to help navigation around the docks.
- A stern chase lamp is the rear light to hang on the barge whilst under tow.
- Seed scoops were used when unloading seed, being shovels with a circular cross-section and raised sides to enable a good shovel-full of seed to be moved into the bucket loaders.

The rope's dimensions are given firstly as length in fathoms with one fathom being equal to six feet, then girth in inches. The largest rope is therefore 150 feet (50 yards, 45 metres) in length, probably made of hemp, and rounded like a well-muscled leg; quite a weight to drag on board when wet, cold, icy or all three.

Although Laurie talks about his work being centred on Alexandra Dock, in Sam's time, *Taurus* worked at many different docks in the Hull area. For instance, whilst on 23 June

Initial inventory for equipment supplied as new with the *Selby Virgo*. Gilyott and Whitakers were Shipping Agents in Hull. (Laurie Dews)

T 242

S. W. & T. COY., LTD.

30/5/22

RIVER CRAFT DEPARTMENT.

DUPLICATE.

Boat *Virgo* Skipper *a Dews*

Joined Ship ___ Left Ship ___

INVENTORY OF STORES ON BOARD.

R 16120

On Joining	PARTICULARS	On Leav'ng	On Joining	PARTICULARS	On Leaving
1	CABIN.—Stove		1	Frosted Lamps	
1	Ashpan *Fender*		2	Side Light Lamps	
1	Rib		1 Set	Boards for Side Lamp and Irons	
1	Poker				
1	Fireshovel		2	Stowers	
1	Bed		2	Boathooks	
2	Pillows				
1	Bolsters		2	Large Anchors and Stocks	
3	Blankets			Small Anchors and Stocks	
1	Quilts		2	Anchor Shackles	
1	Kettle		1	Anchor Davit, complete	
1	Iron Pans, Large		2	Anchor Forelocks with Pin	
1	Iron Pans, Small		2	Cable Chains	
1	Frying Pan		2	Cable Chains Stoppers	
1	Hatchet				
1	Hammer			Small Chains with Padlock and Keys	
1	Marlinspike		2	Handspikes	
1	Moving Spanner		1	Snatch Block	
1	Paraffin Bottle		1	Mop, complete	
1	Water Bucket		2	Hand Brushes	
1	FORECASTLE.—Stove		1	Scrub Brushes	
1	Rib		1	Hold Brushes	
1	Fender		2	Seed Scoops	
1	Poker		2	Iron Handlings	
1	Fireshovel		1	Galvanized Water Tank	
1	Bed		1	Water Dipper	
2	Pillows		2	Galvanized Chimneys	
1	Bolster		1 Set	Steering Board	
3	Blankets		2	Lifebuoys	
1	Quilts		1	Warping Stanchion, complete	
2	Iron Battens for Hatchway			Pestoring Boards	
			1 *Wood*	Iron Battens (set)	
1	Bass Rope, 25 fms., 10 inch		1	Batten Wedges (set)	
1	" 25 " 8 "		2	Wood Tillers	
1	" 17½ " 8 "		4	Pumps and Pump Gear *2 sets*	
2	" 20/5 " 4½ "		2	Cork Fenders	
2	" 20 " 5½ "		1	Cob Boat	
1	Manilla W. 30 " 5 "		1	Boat Oars	
1	Manilla T. 80 " 1½ "		1	Boat Painter	
1	Cotton Rope 40 " 2½ "		1	Boat Chain	
1	Set of Lashings		1	Boat Lock and Key	
1	Rope Fenders		1	Hold Ladder	
1 Pr	Wireman Ropes, complete		1	Fog Horn	
			1	Fog Bell	
6	Bulk Covers		1	Weather Stanchions and Board	
1	Forecastle Hatch Cover		2	Slices	
1	Rope Covers		1	Crowbar	
			2	Windlass Levers	
	Lamp Mast, complete		2	Paint Brushes	
1	Red Lamp			Iron Dredger and Chain	
1	Riding Lamp		2	Tar Brushes	
1	Riding Lamp Stand		1	Paint Buckets	
1	*Stern Lamp*		2	*Padlocks + Keys*	

CHARACTER	ABILITIES
FOR WILLIAM GILYOTT & CO., LTD.	(Agents) Foreman's Signature :—
JOHN H. WHITAKER, LIMITED	On Joining *F. Markham* Date *30/5/22*
LENGTH OF SERVICE	
YEARS MONTHS	On Leaving ___ Date ___

Schematic map of Hull Docks

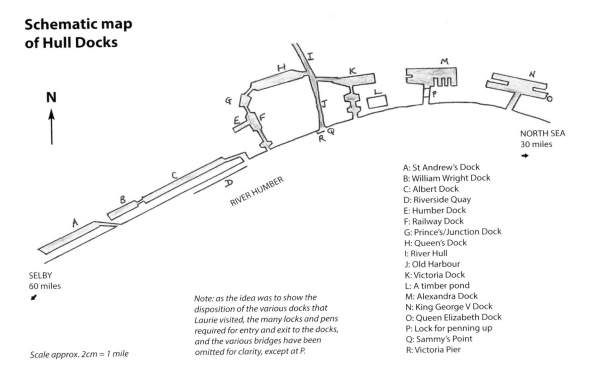

N

SELBY
60 miles

Scale approx. 2cm = 1 mile

RIVER HUMBER

NORTH SEA
30 miles

A: St Andrew's Dock
B: William Wright Dock
C: Albert Dock
D: Riverside Quay
E: Humber Dock
F: Railway Dock
G: Prince's/Junction Dock
H: Queen's Dock
I: River Hull
J: Old Harbour
K: Victoria Dock
L: A timber pond
M: Alexandra Dock
N: King George V Dock
O: Queen Elizabeth Dock
P: Lock for penning up
Q: Sammy's Point
R: Victoria Pier

Note: as the idea was to show the disposition of the various docks that Laurie visited, the many locks and pens required for entry and exit to the docks, and the various bridges have been omitted for clarity, except at P.

Taurus is at Alexandra Dock, on 3 July, having tripped to Selby and back, she is at Victoria Dock. This diagram of the docks in Hull shows the many and various docks available for the bargemen to load and unload cargo at.

Sam's cargo on the first trip on the page is recorded as coal, so either Sam was taking a job outside his work for OCO or was supplying fuel for the factory. The cargo on 22 July is recorded as being 'oil'. Given that the *Taurus* did not have the bulkheads needed to safely carry liquid oil, this oil may have been in barrels, or Sam may have been persuaded to take a risk for extra money, travelling the presumably quiet summertime river. This is a return cargo to Hull, so may have been a 'hardened oil' from the Ardol part of the OCO factory.

From time to time *Taurus* has to be towed from one dock to another in the Hull complex. An example of this happens on 12/13 August.

On 15 August comes some bad economic news; the pay rate is reduced by 1d (½p) per ton. That may seem insignificant, but

Diagram of layout of the docks in Hull.

(Author)

23	6	21	Towed to Hull Alex dock				
24			Settled up freight	13	6	8	2 10
25			Towed to Joint dock tug Mudge				
30			Loaded coal ss Granville firth 160 ton				
1	7	21	Towed to Selby tug City				
2			discharged coal and towed to				
3			Hull Victoria dock				
4			Settled up freight	11	9	11	2 10
5			Started loading ground nut				
			ss Stanya and finished loading				
7			finished up with the Vega and				
			changed over on to the Taurus				
			and started loading				
8			finished the ground nut shut				
11			finished loading Gillyatt no 1 123				
13			towed to Selby tug Robie				
14			discharged nuts	12	0	0	3 0 0
18			Settled up freight				
22			Started loading oil				
23			finished oil 121 tons				
25			towed to Hull tug Robie Humber dock				
27			discharged oil ss Gowrie settled up	8	0	0	1 0 0
2	8		Started loading Rangoon beans				
3			ss Jolly Diana				
3			finished loading Rangoon beans				
6			towed to Selby tug Robie				
8			Discharged beans				
12			towed to Hull tug Robie Alex dock				
13			towed to joint dock and settled up	12	17	5	2 10
15			1s reduction per ton				
16			Started loading black seed				
18			finished				
20			Towed to Selby and smashed Meteor				
			boat up in willow tree reach				
22			Discharged cotton seed and tug left us				
23			towed to Hull tug Robie Victoria dock hit hook bridge				
24			Settled up freight	12	12	9	2 10
27			towed to Albert dock tug Barrow				
29			Started loading black seed ss tigress				
31			finished				
2	9		towed to Selby tug Robie				
3			discharged				
4			towed to Hull joint dock tug Ouse				
5			Settled up freight	13	18	0	2 10
6			Started loading black seed ss				
			Ronald				

Extract from Sam Dews' log, 1921. (Laurie Dews)

The *Selby Taurus* when almost new.

(Laurie Dews)

if the original rate was 1/5 or 17d per ton, that represents a pay cut of over five per cent.

Five days later, there was some more shattering news – this time literally. There seems to have been a collision between the new Taurus and an older dumb barge in the OCO fleet, the *Leeds Meteor*. This happened at Willow Tree Rack, so presumably occurred during 'singling out'. Luckily, the damage does not seem to have been too serious, as no further reports or repairs seem to have been required. The *Meteor* survived to do barge balloon duty in the Second World War. This round trip clearly wasn't a happy one as on 23 August, it's recorded that Taurus hit Hook Bridge on the return trip to Hull.

Perhaps Sam was still getting used to his new craft. Lest all these collisions lead one to believe that these bargemen were very poor helmsmen, one must bear in mind the complexities of steering a barge in the currents and eddies caused by bridge supports.

Taurus was 97ft (30m) long with a 17ft 10in (5.5m) beam. She could carry 200 tons of cargo with a 6ft 8in (2m) draught. The cargo hold had four 'fore and afters', one to each hold, with forty-eight hatchboards on each side and six tarpaulin covers.

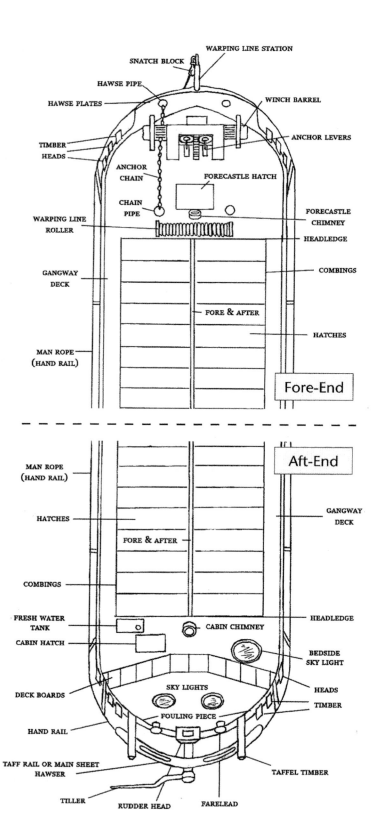

Plan view of the
Selby Taurus.
(Alice Prince)

'Taurus' was 97' (30m) long
with a 17'10" (5.5m) beam

These fitted into batten lugs secured with battin' irons and wooden wedges. The anchor had 30 fathoms (180 feet, 55m) of chain in two equal lengths.

In late January 1922, there was more bad news. A collision with *Robie* caused damage to companion barge *Leeds Solar* in foggy conditions. Obviously, even if the *Solar* crew had a foghorn and fog bell in their inventory, they didn't do their job satisfactorily. Navigating in the dark and foggy conditions must have required strong nerves and tremendous faith in your colleagues.

It is difficult today to comprehend quite how physically and mentally demanding a dumb barge skipper's job was. The captain of the 1920s had none of today's electronic aids and safety devices. Sam had neither radar nor sonar to advise him of the approach of any other vessel on the tide-way, and no GPS to tell him his exact position: that knowledge derived from a waterman's familiarity with his 'route'.

Sam's craft had no power of its own: whilst its motion had to be faster than the tide's velocity to allow the tiller to have effective steerage, that impetus derived entirely from the tug's pull on the tow rope. The helmsman had to exert a strong force on the tiller to counteract the tendency for barges to be drawn together into the tug's wake.

A flotilla going upstream was likely to meet traffic coming down to Hull. The Ouse has many meanders and its banks are high, so that even in daylight it was difficult to detect oncoming traffic. At night time, in fog or in poor visibility, one had to trust to the mate looking out for the ship's lights or listening out for a barge's bell or a ship's foghorn. The jetty at Blacktoft had its own foghorn to add to the sonic confusion. On UK waters, the 'rule of the road' was to pass 'port to port', so as craft approached each other, Sam's barge was steered as far to starboard as was safe.

Added to the complexity of all this manoeuvring was the state of the barge itself. Since it made economic sense to load a barge as fully as possible, it was likely that the freeboard was around six inches. Therefore, any journey between tiller at the rear and lookout at the front to ensure that your cargo, your wages for the next two weeks, was staying dry was carried out along decks likely to be awash with icy water.

3	12	21	loaded 50 tons cake						
4			towed to Hull tug Robie Town dks						
5			discharged, light ss Hull Railway dk	a	13	0		2	10	0
			settled up freights	3	2	6				
6			towed round to Alex dock tug Elsa parten							
			started loading linseed ss Moira							
7			finished " " "							
8			towed to Selby tug Robie discharged							
14			towed to Hull " " " town dks							
15			settled up freights	9	5	10		2	10	0
16			towed to Albert dk.							
30			started loading black sad							
			ss Castilian							

1922

2	1	22	finished loading						
7			towed to Selby tug Elsa parten						
8			arrived at Selby early morning						
10			discharged seed						
11			towed to Hull tug Secker Alex dk	1	5	1	0	2	10
			settled up freight						
12			started loading linseed						
13			finished " "						
14			loaded 100 bags damaged seed						
17			towed to Selby tug Robie						
18			discharged seed. cut the						
			Reg. No 144081 on the beam						
22			towed to Hull tug Robie came						
			foggy boat Solar collided						
			with the tug but a large indent · P bow						
23			settled up freight	12	19	7		2	10	0
26			started loading linseed ss Trevore							
27			finished							
30			towed to Selby tug Secker							
			deduction 1d per ton							
31			discharged linseed							
1	2		towed to Hull Alex dk tug Robie							
2			settled up freight	12	10	1		2	10	
7			started loading linseed							
8			finished 199 tons							
9			towed to Selby tug Robie							
11			discharged linseed							
15			towed to Hull tug Lancelot							
16			landed Hull Albert dok settled up	11	8	11		2	10	0
21			towed round to Alex dock tug Secker							
22			started loading PK ss Sulemna							

Extract from Sam Dews' log, January 1922. (Laurie Dews)

The proverbial cherry on the cake was provided by the tug's exhaust. Either oil- or coal-fired, a regular blast of sulphurous fumes from the chimney acted as a 'livener' for the lungs.

A skipper's financial reward was no more than average for a skilled working man, and during the decade, fiscal conditions worsened. On 30 January, Sam records a reduction of 1d per ton carried, making a 10% reduction in tariffs over a six-month period.

Our next extract takes us forward to 1924, this time to late February.

Things had been continuing in their usual way until 16 February when Bill recorded, 'Start of Big Dock Strike'. This was a dispute between dockers and their employers, to which the bargemen were bystanders. The National Archives record the problem as stated to the Cabinet on 16 February, and the resolution that followed eight days later. Working conditions for dockers were generally very poor. They were usually employed on a casual basis, day by day and had little job security. There was often competition between gangs of dockers, which could sometimes break into violence. In Liverpool, for example, there were teams of Scottish, Irish, Welsh and Manx dockers. Employers could use the rivalry between them to keep wages low. A strike was called in February 1924 when relations between unions and employers reached breaking point. The Minister of Labour made a full statement to the Cabinet as to the circumstances in which the Dock Dispute had been brought within sight of an immediate settlement, and of the terms on which it was hoped that a settlement would be reached. These terms included an increase to the wages of workers of 1/- (5p or £1.50 in 2016 terms) a day at once, and a second 1/- on the first Monday in June, along with certain changes in the terms and conditions of employment.

At the time, dockers were being paid from 11/- to 13/- per day – or about £3 per week (about £100 in 2016 terms, but the £3 figure was slightly above average for a manual worker in 1924). The full pay increase would amount to something in the region of a fifteen per cent hike in pay. This may well represent the industrial power of the dockers; the Government, clearly concerned by the effects this strike could have on the public good had the wage increases not been accepted, prepared plans for the emergency distribution of food.

6	2	24	finished loading ss. Auginia					
7			Towed to Selby tug Robie					
8			Started discharging					
9			finished					
12			Loaded 87 tons cake left Selby					
			tug Robie					
13			Colided with sloop Whitehall					
			in Goole reach and land Hull					
14			Started discharging cake ss Hull					
15			Started discharging cake ss Proffiner barge					
16			finished cake towed to Albert Dock					
			tug Carrow settled up	3	17	6	1	0	0
			Start of big dock Spike					
25			£d per ton Raise in freight					
26			towed to Alex dock tug Cawood					
27			Started loading Linseed ss Tenbury					
28			finished loading					
29			left Hull tug Robie had to return					
			to Hull engine trouble					
			left Hull night tide tug Sesther					
1	3		arrived Selby discharged towed					
			to Hull tug Carrow					
2			arrived Alexandra dock	9	0	2	2	0	0
4			Settled up times					
5			Started loading ss Coulournlinsee					
6			towed to Selby tug Robie					
7			discharged					
8			Started loading cake for Goole 200					
10			finished loading and towed to					
			Goole tug Lancilot					
12			Started discharging					
15			finished discharging and towed					
			to Hull Alex dh tug Goole 4					
17			Settled two freights (linseed) and cake	16	0	7	10	
18			183 197	9	1	0	0	2	0
			Started loading PK ss Eguanga					
20			finished loading					
21			towed to Selby tug Lancilot					
22			discharged towed to Hull					
			Joint dh. tug Lancilot					
24			Started loading Copra ss Yeddo					
25			finished					
26			settled up freight PK 220	10	10	10	2	0	0
27			towed to Selby tug Wilberforce					
28			discharged Copra					

Extract from Sam Dews' log and the strike, 1924. (Laurie Dews)

The bargemen were back at work after nine days, and some of the dockers' gains had been shared by the bargemen, as the entry for 25 February shows an increase in pay rates of ½d (or about two per cent) per ton. Not much, but a step in the right direction. However, a few days later *Robie* broke down and the convoy had to return to Hull, meaning more hire costs for OCO and another long day for Sam as he had to wait for the evening tide.

Moving forward a year to February 1925, we find the *Taurus* falling foul of a hazard that was a common affliction at Selby.

The *Taurus* 'fell athwart' Selby bridge whilst returning empty to the jetty at Selby, to wait for a tug to Hull. Short of sinking, this is possibly the worse fate that can befall a barge. If you hit another craft or a fender at the dock, then provided actions weren't negligent, this is an accident that can be accommodated. A few dents in a steel ship weren't fatal and Hull had a Dry Dock where repairs could be swiftly carried out. Both bridges and barges had meaty fenders so some collisions might be more sound than fury. Even running aground wasn't always a disaster. Although you could be trapped on a sand bank and risk the back of the barge breaking as the river level fell, a pull from the tug or fixing a rope on a tree on the bank and pulling hard might get you off. But once a barge had fallen athwart or across a bridge you were stuck there for the duration of the tide, with its force exacerbating any damage that might have been caused by the original collision.

But how could experienced helmsmen make such a mistake? It's all down to the difficulties of navigation caused by how the presence of a large object – in this case the stanchions of a bridge – affects the flow of a river.

The barges generally came upriver with the tide. It is clearly an advantage to work with the tide rather than against it, but it does have implications for the speed at which the barge travels. The barges didn't just 'surf' on the tide. If it was as simple as that there would be no need for the tug.

The convoy had to be travelling more rapidly than the tide was flowing to have what the bargemen called steerage – that is, to allow the rudder to have an effect on the direction of travel as they made headway through the water.

Whilst travelling along a rack the tiller work was fairly straightforward – keep the bow pointing ahead, but hold hard onto

18. 2. 25		finished loading			
19		Towed to Selby tug Robie			
23		discharged			
24		Started loading cake			
25		finished . . . . dropped athwart			
		the bridge			
26		towed to Hull tug J. Rymer			
27		Settled up 63 tons beans 154 Lombax 5 days	14	11	0
28		discharged 30 tons oil 11 mundes			
1	3	Alteration in working condition			
2		discharged cake settled up	6	14	11
		Started ground nuts SS Selby			
3		finished nuts			
4		towed to Albert dock tug Yoga			
5		Started loading nuts 11 Albatross			
6		towed to Alex dock tug barrow			
		Started loading PK			
7		finished loading 11 Ghana			
9		towed to Selby tug Robie			
13		discharged			
15		towed to Hull tug Robie	13	12	4
16		Settled up 205 tons 5 days 1 sunday		10	0
		Started loading			
17		loading PK 11 Gambia			
23		Started loading ground nuts SS			
		SS Othello.			
24.		finished loading.			
26.		Towed to Selby tug Seeker.			
29.		Started Discharging.			
30.		finished Discharging. Started loading PK			
31.		finished Loading & towed to Hull. Seeker			
apil 1st		Settled up 213 tons 8 8 days 1	15	11	11
3		Started Discharging cake SS. Otto.			
6.		finished Discharging. S.S. Hull.			
		Settled up 108 tons 8 1 day	5	15	1
7.		Started loading PK SS Harrogate			
8		finished ship PK and ground nuts			
9		towed round to Alexandra Dock			
		tug wilberforce			
15.		Started loading fullersearth SS Thurlin			
16		finished loading fullersearth			
17		Towed to Selby Tug Lancelot			
18		Started discharging fullersearth			
20		finished			
21		Discharged PK. & started loading oil			

Extract from Sam Dews' log 1925. Going athwart. (Laurie Dews)

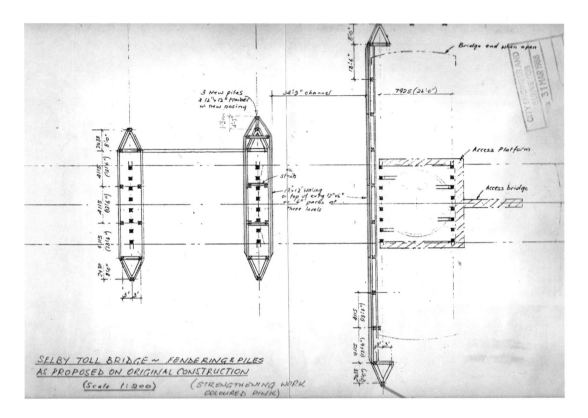

SELBY TOLL BRIDGE ~ FENDERING & PILES
AS PROPOSED ON ORIGINAL CONSTRUCTION
(Scale 1:200)   (STRENGTHENING WORK COLOURED PINK)

Engineer's Drawing of
clearances at Selby
Toll Bridge, 1988.
(Author)

the tiller to stop the wake from the tug pushing the barges too far apart. Rounding bends in the river meant a slight adjustment to the tiller, but nothing out of the ordinary. However, once you approach a bridge, the water flow is affected by the bridge supports. In a similar way to the way in which an airplane wing generates lift because air is flowing faster over the top surface of the wing than the bottom, different speeds and directions of water flow create unbalanced forces on the barge's bow.

Here the increased force on the starboard bow tends to push the barge towards the pillar. The tillerman would have to move the tiller to the right so that the barge was steered towards starboard to counteract this effect. This required muscle power and a bit of common sense, but normally simple bridges like Hook Bridge and Barmby Bridge could be passed relatively easily.

Unfortunately, Selby has two bridges in close proximity, being separated by merely 200 yards. From a bargeman's point of view this is tricky territory indeed. The difficulty of the

Diagrammatic representation of how currents can make a barge go athwart. (Author)

passage is heightened still further by the way in which the river has narrowed, exacerbating the effects of any current. A successful passage of the bridge requires the piloting of a twenty-foot-wide barge through a thirty-five-foot-wide gap, as shown by the Engineer's diagram of 1988.

Whilst the bridge has more than one gap between its pillars, to attempt to take a barge through anything other than the central opening span was certain disaster. The current flow and potential problems can be summed up in the text and diagram below.

Once successfully past the 'normal' navigational problem of the rail bridge with its single pillar, as at A, a course slightly

Going athwart

Ignoring the tug's wash and under normal conditions, with the barge going directly ahead, there's equal force on each side of the bow, so the man on the tiller has to keep the tiller dead ahead.

When an object like a bridge pillar interrupts the flow, there's a lower-pressure area beyond the pillar, which the bridge could be pushed towards. If it's a pillar to starboard, he man on the tiller to starboard, to force the barge to go to port and so keep straight. The opposite argument would apply for a port-side pillar.

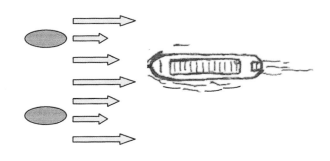

If the turning movement isn't corrected, and the barge starts making an angle with the bridge, (A), things have gone too far. The currents will turn the barge across the river (B), with the inevitable collision (C). The barge is now athwart the bridge.

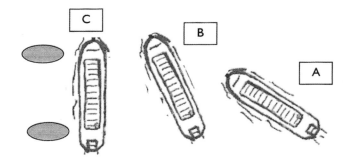

across the river had to be set to approach the open span of the Toll Bridge. However, that left the barge open to lateral forces from the river, turning the bow around (as at B).

This could be resisted by stout work on tiller and tug, but if the angle became too great, things had gone beyond human control. The barge would be turned to lay across the river, and as this was happening the tow rope would be struck off. The barge now had no steerage and was merely a 200ton, 100-foot-long stick being propelled on the tide towards a thirty-five foot wide gap. Bang!

Going athwart was about the worst navigational crime a barge skipper could commit. His barge would be trapped against the bridge whilst the tide flowed; at least five hours when nothing could be done to earn money. Damage to either barge or bridge would result in financial loss to either company or captain. Finally, there was the risk of loss of cargo or even sinking of the barge should the currents make the craft turn turtle. Beyond those considerations were the effects on transport through Selby. Closure of the bridge meant a major north-south road link was blocked, and pedestrian and public transport access between

Here is the *Risby* trapped across Selby Toll Bridge on the Barlby side in December 1979. She was not part of the BOCM fleet, but going athwart was a concern for any vessel. Although she looks to be in a bad way here, after being freed by the tide, she survived to remain in cargo-carrying service (although not for BOCM) until at least 2001.
(Richard Moody)

24	4	Started discharged cake ss York			
26		finished " " cake " "			
27		settled up 125 tons cake joint dock before	6	3	8
1		Started loading ground nuts City of Paris			
4		General Strike begun			
7		settled			
8		loading			
9		finished loading			
10		towed to Selby tug Robie			
11		discharged nuts			
12		loaded cake towed to Hull tug Lancelot			
		and collided with Feethams lighter			
		Beatrice at tug jetty about 10 P.m			
23		arrived Hull Victoria dock			
25		discharged 100 tons cake Coast			
26		" " " 44 2 cases ss l atora			
		settled up freight 207 tons 1 day	12	7	9
		139 "	6	19	0
27		left 39 tons cake return to Selby towed			
		Alex dock canwood			
28		Started loading linseed ss Alantica			
31		finished loading			
1	5	Towed to Selby tug Robie 2 stowers 1 tiller			
		washed overboard			
7		discharged seed started loading oil			
9		finished loading left Selby tug Robie			
10		lost boat Howden dyke arrived in Hull			
11		discharged oil ss Estans Started loading			
12		Settled up linseed 225 tons 5 day	14	5	0
14		" " oil down 164 tons	8	4	0
16		finished loading cotton seed ss Manana			
25		towed to Selby tug Robie			
26		Discharged seed			
27		towed to Hull Alex dock tug J. Rymer			
		collided with lighter and put small indent			
		on port side, in Alex dock entrance			
28		Settled up 201 tons 9 days Bombay cotton	16	7	0
30		Started loading linseed ss gambia River			
		paid mate off Sam Sissons			
2	6	finished loading linseed			
5		towed to Selby tug Lancelot			
9		discharged seed Started loading cake			
10		finished loading cake Victory jetty			
11		towed to Hull tug Lancelot			
12		Settled up 223 tons linseed	12	7	2
		Started discharging " Hull			

Extract from Sam Dews' log, 1926. (Laurie Dews)

Selby, Barlby and beyond to York greatly restricted. The situation was only resolved at the cessation of the tide.

In the log entry of 1 March, a 'change in working conditions' is recorded. As this is almost exactly a year since the dock strike of 1924 referred to above, perhaps this is an echo of the resolution of that dispute. The next extract covering the period April to June 1926 is full of incident, with different kinds of strikes.

On 4 May, Sam records that the General Strike had begun; in response to a specific case of hardship endured in the coal mining industry, a General Strike was called. Many manual and transport workers 'downed tools' but unlike in the 1924 Dock Strike, the government did not offer pay increases and the walkout fizzled out after nine days. Returning to work on 18 May, it was not long before there was another collision with the *Beatrice*, and on presumably 1 June (although the log has it as being May) both stowers and the tiller are washed overboard, and nine days later, the boat (presumably the cob boat) is lost at Howdendyke. Mate Sam Sissons clearly had had enough as he was paid off on 30 May.

Our next extracts are from the autumn of 1927. Just two brief extracts to show how major incidents were recorded in the tersest possible way.

October seems to have started in a normal way, but there was a burglary, with a minor but important loss recorded on Monday 3 October. From time to time, skippers would secure their craft and go home to Hull or Selby. Perhaps this was done after

Extract from Sam Dews' log, Oct. 1927. (Laurie Dews)

Extract from Sam Dews' log, Nov. 1927.
(Laurie Dews)

discharging and settling up, and Sam took a Sunday away from the Docks, but the cabin wasn't as secure as he thought. It was unlikely that either Sam or OCO had taken out what we might think of today as 'contents insurance', so replacements would come out of the wages.

The *Selby Pollux* (written *Polax* here) was primarily an oil tanker, so may well have sunk as a result of her cargo shifting making the barge roll over. The *Pollux* must have been refloated after this incident, as Laurie's mate Johnny Roddam was on it in one of their wartime adventures. As the page from 1928 shows, the handwriting has changed, indicating a fresh author for the log. The writing is certainly easier on the eye, and shows the wide variety of cargoes and tugs that the Dews' vessel was involved with. There are at least eight tugs and five different cargoes described, including soot and oil.

Looking at the pay rate for the cargo that was settled up on 19 July, it was now down to 1/2 (6p) per ton, a marked reduction from earlier in the decade.

On 25 August, payment for painting the barge is recorded. Spring 1931 saw the barge laid up for almost a month. As it was around ten years since the Dews took delivery of the *Taurus*, perhaps this was a ten-year 'check up', or perhaps 'survey' and 'repairs' hints at some kind of accident linked to an insurance claim.

The crew was paid for this down time – albeit not at the same rate as for voyages. In all £10/17/6 is paid for twenty-nine days in dry dock. A tragedy occurred around Christmas 1931. A new mate, C. Wreathall had been taken on in the autumn. Coming up to Christmas – when the bargemen normally had a few days' holiday – he was paid just over £4/8/- wages, a good amount to see Christmas in with.

```
June 19"   settled up   47 tons                              2 · 7 · 10
June 26.   found the cog boat in joint Dock
July 2.    loaded 100 bags of soot SS His.
  — 3.     Towed to alexandra Dock Jug AGETUT
           started loading Bombay cotton seed
           SS. Lawbeach
  — 5       finished loading
  — 6       Towed to Selby Jug LANCELOT
  — 7       Discharged cotton seed
  — 9       Discharged soot
  — 11      Towed to Hull Jug LANCELOT          11· 6· 1
           settled up
  — 16      Started loading Bombay cotton seed
           S.S. WAR NURURTON.
  — 17      finished loading Towed to Selby Jug LANCELOT.
  — 18      Discharged cotton seed Towed to Hull
           Jug SEEKER alexandra Dock            11· 7· 10
  — 19      settled up 194 Tons Bombay
  — 20      Started loading Bombay S.S KATE.
  — 23      finished loading
  — 24      Towed to Selby Jug ROBIE.
  — 31      Discharged cotton seed
aug. 1      stopped at Railway Jetty Jug
           broke down
  — 2       Towed to Hull Jug ROBIE Alex Dock
  — 3       Settled up 210 tons Bombay cotton seed
           and 5 days.                          14·11·10
  — 8       Started loading ground nuts
  — 20      Towed to Selby Jug LANCELOT
  — 24      Discharged nuts
  — 25      Towed to Hull joint Dock settled
           up nut 209 tons 10 days              16· 3· 11
               Painting money.                   6· 0· 0
  — 27      started loading linseed
  — 28      finished ship..
  — 29      Started linseed again S.S DILMENTON.
  — 30      finished the Ship.
Sept 3     Towed to Selby Jug LANCELOT.
  — 11      Discharged linseed. Started loading
           case oil.
  — 12      finished loading cake and oil
  — 13      Towed to Hull Jug LANCELOT. Alex Dock
  — 14      Discharged 180 cases SS IDAHO. and
           Towed to Harbour Jug WILBER FORCE.
  — 15      Started Discharged cake B.O.C.M.
           Drypool warehouse
```

Extract from Sam Dews' log, in a different hand, 1928. (Laurie Dews)

Belled 1 761 tons copra 129
oak 3 days H. H. 0
May 22nd Surveying by insurance.
Came out of dry dock and
laid out side to finish
repairs
23 Finished at (dry) dock yard
and towed to Alex dock tug
cawood.   11.14.0

21st started discharging oil and cake
s.s Otto
Settled up 173 copra 1000
mate C Wreathall 33 2   3.32
                                           10.0
23 finished discharging oil s.s Feano
settled up £1 2 0 tons   6.0..0
                      sunday   10..0
26th mate fell paid C Wreathall   1.5.0
drowned C Wreathall
30th Towed to joint dock tug
W home

Top to Bottom:

Extract from Sam
Dews' log. (Laurie Dews)

A tragic entry in Sam
Dews' log. (Laurie Dews)

A new year entry in
Sam Dews' log.
(Laurie Dews)

Whether he saw Christmas in too well will never be known, but his sad demise on Boxing Day is recorded, again without ceremony. The elongated holidays that now seem commonplace around Christmas certainly didn't apply in the 1930s. It was back to work after, at best, a couple of days – and nothing special for New Year's Day.

Overleaf is the tale for December 1933, and we are in familiar territory. Problems with the weather, problems with tugs, loading and unloading, and managing to get finished for Christmas.

Jan 1 started loading C African cotton
towed to Alex dock from
joint dock tug cawood

1932
1-1-32 Started loading C African Cotton
s.s Montula
towed to alex dock tug Kong lit
                      2 tides
                      C. Laurence   0.14.0

c	12	Towed to Hull Joint Dock tug W. force
	13	Started Loading Linseed S.S. Magdunfim
	14	Loading
	15	Finished Loading
	16	No Tug
	18	Left Hull Landed Blacktoft tug Lancelot Fog all day
	19	Arrived Selby Discharged Left Selby Landed Gorle
		Fog Bound tug Lancelot New Tow Rope 2 gall Paraffin
	20	Fog Stayed at Goole
	22	Landed Hull P.M. alex Dock
	23	Settle up 187 tons Linseed.
	29	Started Loading Black seed S.S. Penast
	30	Loading.
1934		
Jan	1	Finished Loading.

8 - 4 - 1 (

Final entries in Sam Dews' log book 1933/34. (Laurie Dews)

Laurie as a schoolboy, at an age when he would have begun taking trips on Sam's barge. The Selby Abbey school cap shows the 'Three Swans' badge of Selby. (Laurie Dews)

For no apparent reason, the log concludes abruptly on 1 January 1934, and thirteen years of re-cording the daily trials and tribulations of barge skipper and his charge come to an end.

At the start of 1934, Laurie was ten years old. Whilst no examples of Sam carrying him, brother Frank and Mam Elisabeth on board are recorded, and indeed Sam might have been in trouble with the company if such a voyage had been known to officialdom, Laurie was now of an age when the family outings down to Hull in the summer holidays could begin.

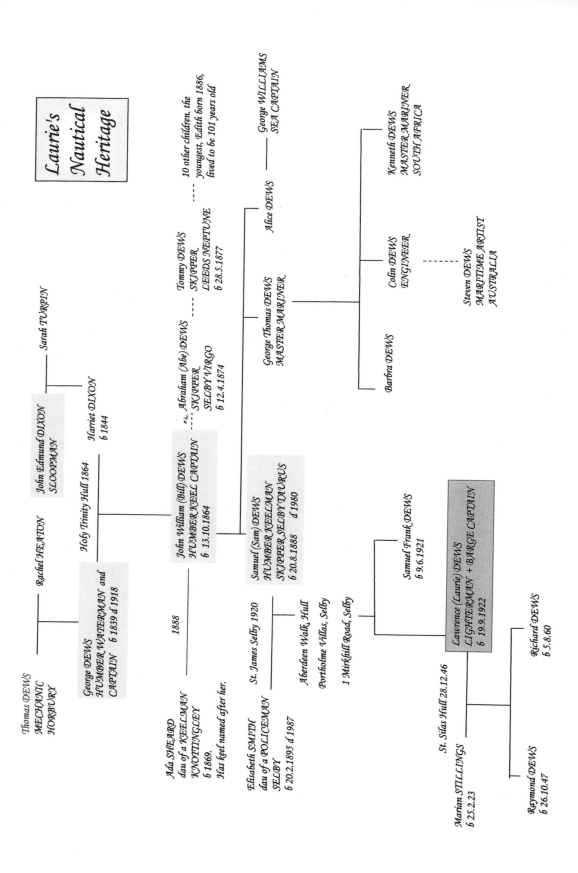

Laurie's Nautical Heritage

Thomas DEWS
MECHANIC
HORBURY

Rachel HEATON — George DEWS
HUMBER WATERMAN and
CAPTAIN
b 1839 d 1918

John Edmund DIXON
SLOOPMAN — Sarah TURPIN

Holy Trinity Hull 1864

Harriet DIXON
b 1844

John William (Bill) DEWS
HUMBER KEEL CAPTAIN
b 13.10.1864

Abraham (Abe) DEWS
SKIPPER,
SELBY VIRGO
b 12.4.1874
---- Tommy DEWS
SKIPPER
LEEDS NEPTUNE
b 28.5.1877

10 other children, the
youngest, Edith born 1886,
lived to be 101 years old

George Thomas DEWS
MASTER MARINER

Alice DEWS — George WILLIAMS
SEA CAPTAIN

Barbra DEWS

Colin DEWS
ENGINEER

Kenneth DEWS
MASTER MARINER
SOUTH AFRICA

Steven DEWS
MARITIME ARTIST
AUSTRALIA

Ada SHEARD
dau of a KEELMAN
KNOTTINGLEY
b 1869.
Has keel named after her.

1888

Elisabeth SMITH
dau of a POLICEMAN
SELBY
b 20.2.1895 d 1987

St. James Selby 1920

Samuel (Sam) DEWS
HUMBER KEELMAN
SKIPPER SELBY TAURUS
b 20.8.1888   d 1980

Aberdeen Walk, Hull
Portholme Villas, Selby
1 Mirkhill Road, Selby

Samuel Frank DEWS
b 9.6.1921

Laurence (Laurie) DEWS
LIGHTERMAN + BARGE CAPTAIN
b 19.9.1922

Marian STILLINGS
b 25.2.23

St. Silas Hull 28.12.46

Reymond DEWS
b 26.10.47

Richard DEWS
b 5.8.60

Chapter 4

HOW THE DEWS FAMILY CAME TO WORK ON THE RIVER

To begin the story of Laurie's career on the river, study of his family tree shows that he was almost destined to have a career there. It is clear that Laurie had 'boatman's blood' going back four generations and almost 200 years. Laurie is described as a 'lighterman' and 'barge captain'. The latter job description is obvious, but the term 'lighterman' perhaps needs some explanation. Lightermen are involved in the 'alighting' of goods, using that word in the same archaic sense encountered when passengers are asked to 'alight' from a bus or train at a stop or station. People move from one mode of carriage to another. On the docks, the craft such men work on is deemed a 'lighter', a flat-bottomed cargo-containing dumb barge, restricted to work in a dock complex. In the Dews family case this might involve transferring goods between one craft in Alexandra Dock and a different one in Victoria Dock. As Laurie was involved in movements like this with barges like *Taurus*, it's accurate to state that he was a lighterman.

The rivers of Yorkshire have carried trade between the workshops of the West Riding and the fields of the East Riding to and from the ports on the East Coast for centuries. Laurie's family is one of dozens that were involved in this business.

Not only were the Dews family involved on the water, they lived close to it. As well as the obvious links to the Humber at Hull and the Ouse at Selby, Horbury, near Wakefield is on the River Calder. The Knottingley roots of the family were close to the Aire and Calder Canal. In the nineteenth century, the Dews family boatmen seem to have been available to take cargoes to many parts of the waterway network of this part of Yorkshire, having been recorded as taking cargoes to Wakefield and Leeds, Sheffield and Gainsborough. In the nineteenth century, craft were not the dumb barges pulled by tugs that were Laurie's father's

OPPOSITE:
Extracts from Laurie Dews' family tree.
(Laurie Dews)

Schematic map of canals and rivers linked to the Dews family

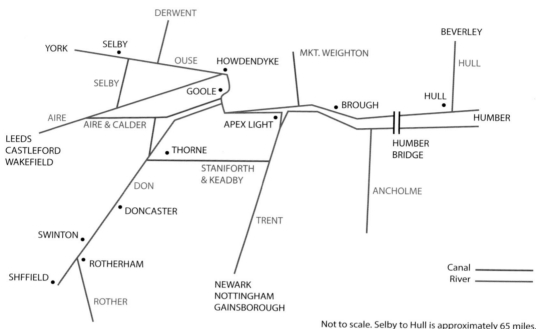

Not to scale. Selby to Hull is approximately 65 miles. The rivers have many more meanders than shown.

Schematic diagram of the waterways worked by the Dews family. (Author)

vessel of choice. Instead, Bill and before him George, and before him Thomas depended on the power of the wind and when the wind didn't blow, the haulage effort of a horse. These craft were keels and sloops, hence Laurie's forebears' job descriptions.

Keels and sloops worked on the inland waterways in the nineteenth and early twentieth centuries, both ideally suited to the Humber and its associated waterways of narrow creeks and treacherous sand bars. They were highly manoeuvrable, with a very shallow draft, being able to work in as little as three feet of water. A Humber keel could carry around fifty tons of cargo. The major difference was in the rigging of the sails. Keels are thought to be derived from the Viking longship that would have ventured up the Humber in the days before the Norman Conquest and were first noted in the fourteenth century as a vessel called a 'Keyll'. Their sail is suspended symmetrically

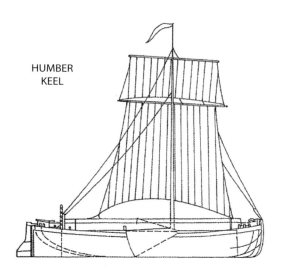

HUMBER
KEEL

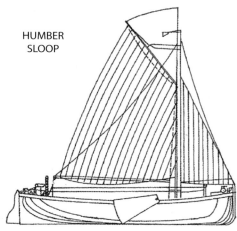

HUMBER
SLOOP

from the mast. A sloop had a boom so that the sail could project beyond the boat, and also had a foresail.

When navigating canals, the mast could be detached and left at certain locations to avoid fouling canal bridges. Once this was done, horsepower was vital. If a horse was not available, sometimes human power had to be pressed into service.

Although somewhat shorter than Laurie's 100-foot-long barges, keels and sloops had several features that he would have recognized. These included: 'stowers'; boathooks and warping lines used for heaving the craft around in docks and narrow waterways; a water dipper and anchors that could be used for steering as well as securing a mooring.

Family life on board revolved around a cosy cabin with a separate, smaller cabin for a mate. Whilst the cabin may have been cosy, the working day was full of hard manual labour.

Laurie's great-grandfather George became a Humber keelman around 1860 and married Harriet Dixon, of another Hull boating family, the Turpins, in 1864. George and Harriet went on to have thirteen children. The first child was John William – known as Bill. He was born in late 1864 and married Ada Sheard, daughter of yet another nautical family, this time from Knottingley, when he was twenty-four years old. Bill and Ada had three children, Samuel, Thomas and Alice. All three followed in the maritime tradition. Daughter Alice married a sea captain, George Williams,

Diagram of the outline of a sloop and a keel.

Examples of the Humber Keel and Sloop. The top image shows a keel being hauled by muscle power. This is probably staged, as if there was no wind to catch the sails, they would have been furled. The lower image, a painting by Reuben Chappell of the sloop 'Lillian', shows how by rigging the sails differently, wind power could be harnessed from several directions, unlike with the keel. This allowed sloops to tack upriver, and so make progress irrespective of the state of the tide, whilst keels could only drift with the tide if they had no following wind.

(Top: Yorkshire Waterways Museum. Lower: Goole Museum)

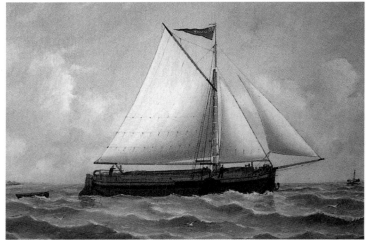

A Dews family group in Hull in 1935. Back row: brother Frank, cousin Kenneth and Laurie. Middle: Ada and Bill Dews. Bottom: Cousins Colin and Barbra and Roland, son of George Williams and Alice Dews.
(Laurie Dews)
See also Laurie's 'family tree' page 64.

Postcard view of the reach at Goole - where Sam Dews had a narrow escape when a babe in arms.
(Susan Butler/ Howdenshire History)

COPYRIGHT
GLF 8

GOOLE REACH

LILYWHITE LTD
BRIGHOUSE

whilst Thomas went to sea and obtained his master's certificate, but the story continues with Laurie's dad, Samuel, or Sam as he was always known.

The first keel that Bill owned was also named Sam, and was involved in an incident that, had it have gone differently, would have meant that there would have been none of Laurie's stories to tell – and indeed, no Laurie.

'Once when Sam was very young and on board with Bill and Ada the Sam *was moored alongside of Goole dock with a load of silk, waiting to pen up. A steam-powered coaster dropped heavily alongside of them, crushing her timber sides and loosing her mooring ropes. Being a wooden keel,* Sam *started to sink. Whilst she was sinking and drifting upstream with the tide topside of Goole jetty, Ada wrapped Sam in a shawl and threw him as a valuable parcel ashore to people stood on the jetty at Shuffleton. Bill and Ada managed to escape in the cob boat.'*

Whilst all three survived the incident, the vessel was less fortunate and was damaged beyond repair. But not much was ever wasted back then and *Sam*'s hulk found a use as Laurie will tell later. A more pressing problem was for Bill to try to regain the value of his keel so that he could begin trading with a new boat.

Painting of the keel *Ada Dews* by Goole maritime artist Reuben Chappell.
(University of Hull Art Collection: Pettifer Collection)

'Bill lost the insurance claim because they said in court that the ship wasn't moored properly, as it was only tied up with a head rope and no stern rope. Bill claimed she was tied up like that because he was about to go into port and the tide would keep her alongside to the jetty. But the court said that didn't alter the fact that he wasn't moored properly so Bill lost the case and any chance of compensation.'

Bill managed to find himself a new keel, named after his wife, the *Ada Dews*.

Sam followed in the family trade and became a Humber keelman, and around the turn of the twentieth century, when Sam was thirteen, he went mate on the *Ada Dews* with Bill.

The *Ada Dews* carried cargo on the Humber and Ouse and also through to Sheffield via the canals and up to Leeds on the Aire and the Aire and Calder Canal. When Sam went mate, his mother Ada could stay at home and look after the family.

But before we continue with Sam's story, Laurie has memories of other family members from Bill's generation.

'Bill's youngest sister was Edith. She was born in 1886, lived until she was 101, so I knew her too. She had a wonderful memory, and told us tales of life on board with my great-grandfather.'

Laurie Dews pictured in 2016 with the 'paying out pennant' from the *Ada Dews*, which was only to be flown on the keel's maiden and final voyages. (Laurie Dews)

Edith had been born on board a barge moored at Victoria Dock on the River Hull.

'When times were good, they hired a horse to pull the boat along the canal. However, if times were hard, the barge was pulled by person power. Edith and her father would take it in turns to put on a leather harness and pull the barge along stretches of the canal.'

Two of Bill's brothers were also on the boats. They were Abraham – or Uncle Abe – and Uncle Tommy. Laurie met them as a lad when they had been working the river for most of their lives, and they made quite an impression on him.

'Uncle Abe had a proper Yorkshire accent, or as we called it, he was a bit "short-tongued". One day I was working mate with him in Alexandra Dock, and his wife Polly was on board, so we needed a bit of water to make things look proper. In those days, the only way to get fresh water was to hang a bucket on your boat hook, and the water boatman would come alongside and fill you up for sixpence. I always remember what Abe asked me to do. He told me, "Go fetch t'watter boat to fill t'watter tank – tell him I've got t'wife on board for t'weekend."'

As for Tommy, Laurie remembers him being 'sharp' in two ways.

'Uncle Tommy was a gent. Skipper of the Leeds Neptune, *he always wore a bowler hat. He'd spend nights in the cabin with the oil light burning, smoking his pipe and telling me his wonderful sailor's tales. I'd be on board, sat in the cabin, me on one side and Uncle Tom on the other. Every so often, he'd take out the pipe, give a little cough and spit at the fire. He never missed! Always the same fire bar, and always the same satisfying sizzling sound when that hot bar was hit.'*

Not surprisingly, these old salts knew a trick or two to make the most of anything the boat owners would give them. One way of stretching the wages came into play when it was time to refurbish the boats.

*'Tom was also a crafty old b****! Every year, the barges had to be painted, and it was the captain's job to see it was done. The company supplied brushes and paint, but the skipper got paid eight guineas (£8.40 or around £200 today) for the job, which was very good money indeed.'*

In the early 1930s, a bargeman's annual pay was around £150, so this payment for doing the painting was about a fortnight's pay, or perhaps working two return trips between Hull and Selby. It was certainly a sum of money worth having, however hard painting a 100-foot long barge might have been.

'The ship's side had to be tarred and everything from the waterline upwards was to be painted, including inside the cabin and fo'c'sle, which were by far the most difficult to do. When you got to Selby, you told the jetty foreman that the job was done, and the transport managers would come down to inspect, and pay the money if the job was good.'

The company livery was for the exterior of the barges to be blue and red above a black-tarred hull.

'So, Uncle Tom would open a tin of blue, paint everything he could and throw the tin away. Then he'd do the same with a tin of red. On arriving at Selby, he'd announce that he was ready to be checked. In due course, the manager came to look around the Neptune. *When he asked if he could look down in the cabin, Tom said, "I wouldn't go down there if I were you – the paint's not dry yet." The blue and red paint on the top part of the boat looked new so the manager guessed the rest must have been done too, passed the* Neptune *and Tom got the money without having to do the hardest part of the painting.'*

Those reminiscences have taken us forward to the 1930s, so it is now appropriate to go back and fill in the thirty years before that. With the coming of the First World War in Europe, it might have been thought that a cargo boatman might be considered a 'reserved occupation' and be protected from the 'call up' as they delivered vital supplies. Although Bill tried to argue this case, the army didn't see it that way, and Sam was called to the colours.

'Granddad Bill wasn't one to stay at home, and declaring that if he couldn't work with his lad on the Ouse, said, "If he goes, I go," and went to sea on Spillers' barges between Hull and Whitby.

'When the war was over, granddad became skipper of the Leeds Eclipse and Sam went skipper of the Selby Vega, brand new from Beverley in 1919. She was one of the final four oil-carrying barges, Vega, Castor, Pollux and Lyra.'

Sam married Laurie's mother, Elisabeth, the daughter of a policeman, in 1920 when he was skipper of the Vega. For a short while, she used to journey up and down the river with him. They had quite a few hair-raising experiences.

'Once, whilst being towed full, down to Hull, it came in foggy off Hessle and the tug ran aground. Now because Vega was "dumb" with no power of her own, when the tug ran aground, the tow rope went slack and there was nothing to keep her going in the right direction. Sam and Elisabeth were at the mercy of the current – not a good situation when you're loaded up with 200 tons of animal feed, you can't see what's coming and you've got no engine. The only control you have is the use of the tiller. So, Sam "knocked off" the tow rope to let the Vega drift downstream but the strength of the current was so great that the tiller did a bit of its own "knocking off". A violent swing of the tiller pushed Sam over the barge's aft rail. As Sam was wearing heavy sailor's boots and a big overcoat, he was odds-on to sink in the Humber without a trace, especially since, despite all his years on the river, he couldn't swim. Sheer luck meant Sam's flailing left hand managed to grasp the aft rail and Elisabeth managed to haul a bedraggled hubby back aboard. He had the presence of mind to grab the tiller to steer the barge into the bank to await a pick up from the tug before going below to warm and dry through in front of the fire.'

Women helped to look after the welfare of the boats with some sharp wit, too. There was often a bit of a free-for-all around the

Mam Elisabeth Dews (née Smith) on right, and her sister, Mary.

(Laurie Dews)

docks. When it came to keeping things tidy, sometimes deckhands weren't so keen where the rubbish was swept. You had to be prepared to give as good as you got.

'One day a narrowboat was moored next to a large coaster. The woman on board the narrowboat was in the cabin when she heard a thump on deck. Coming out of the cabin she saw a pile of rubbish on her deck and a deckhand with a broom in his hand on the freighter high above. "Oi! You get yourself down here and clear up this mess," she shouted up, but the deckhand ignored her cries.

'More shouting brought an officer on deck, looking all officious and with plenty of scrambled egg around his cap. "What seems to be the matter madam?"

'"What's the matter? What's the matter?? Your lad has just swept your rubbish onto my deck and I want him down here right now to clear it all up!"

'"Madam, please don't speak like that. Do you know who you are talking to? I'm the mate of this ship and I'm second in charge after the captain."

'"So?" came the triumphant reply, "I'm the mate of **this** ship, and I **sleep** with the captain!"

'The deckhand meekly came down and cleaned up the mess.'

Elisabeth didn't spend much longer crewing for Sam as Laurie's elder brother Frank was born on 9 June 1921 and Laurie himself followed the next year, on 19 September.

Chapter 5

A CHILDHOOD IN SELBY AND HOLIDAYS ON THE RIVER

After a bit of a struggle to find a place where everyone was happy, Sam and Elisabeth settled down in Selby. Laurie then enjoyed an active childhood, with plenty of exercise and fresh air.

'Mam and Dad bought a house in Aberdeen Street in Hull, but didn't settle. We moved to Portholme Villas in the centre of Selby and went to Selby Abbey School. Sam and Elisabeth moved again to 1, Mirkhill Road, a little further out of town, but we still went to Selby Abbey school. You got fit in them days – we'd walk to school in the morning, then come lunchtime we'd walk back home again cos we had ninety minutes for lunch then back again for the afternoon and another mile or so to get home at the end of the day at four o'clock. Best part of five miles walking every day! When we were a bit older, me brother got a pushbike and he'd crossbar me all the way to school and back.'

If you were growing up in Selby in the twenties and thirties you met a bunch of mates that stayed with you for life.

'You'd go to school and pal about with a bunch of mates, and after school and you'd had your tea you'd be out in the street playing about or round each other's house. Didn't matter what job you went into after school, there would always be that friendship to call on.'

Lads were always interested in what was going on around town. In the 1930s, Selby was on the railway East Coast Main Line, with all the famous expresses that thundered through.

'If we were in town and we heard that special whistle of the Silver Jubilee *we'd run to the station, get on the bridge and be there when it went under. All that steam and smell and noise as it clanked over the bridge. We saw the* Flying Scotsman *too.'*

HIPPODROME, SELBY

Western SOUND **Electric** SYSTEM

Week commencing JANUARY 16th, 1933.

Monday to Friday, Continuous 6-30 to 10-30. Saturday, Two Distinct Houses, at 6-30 and 8-30. Monday, Matinee 2 p.m. Saturday, Matinee 2-30.

MONDAY, TUESDAY, WEDNESDAY.

ISOBEL ELSOM in ILLEGAL

A Sensational British Drama with New and Popular Songs.

THURSDAY, FRIDAY, SATURDAY.

JAMES CAGNEY in

WINNER TAKE ALL

The Most Terrific Actional Picture of the Prize Ring.

Book your Seats Now at SWIFT'S, MILLGATE. Tel. 107.
Next Week: JEWEL ROBBERY and FIREMAN, SAVE MY CHILD.

A cinema advert from the Selby Times of 1933 – the kind of entertainment that Laurie and his mates could enjoy at a matinee.

Selby had various cinemas that showed the favourites of the day as well as having live music- hall type acts.

'Of a Saturday afternoon me and me mates used to go to the cinema for the matinee. It were great fun. A proper afternoon out for just sixpence. We'd get in for about tuppence then we could buy five aniseed balls for a ha'penny - so we'd sit in the back of the cinema eating our sweets and watching the film. When we came out, if it'd been a cowboy we'd all start chasing around slapping our backsides making out we were cowboys on horseback. Marvellous fun!'

Although the houses in and around Mirkhill Road are quite modest Victorian terraces, going in to town on Flaxley Road there were much larger properties, and turning away from town

Outline map of SELBY

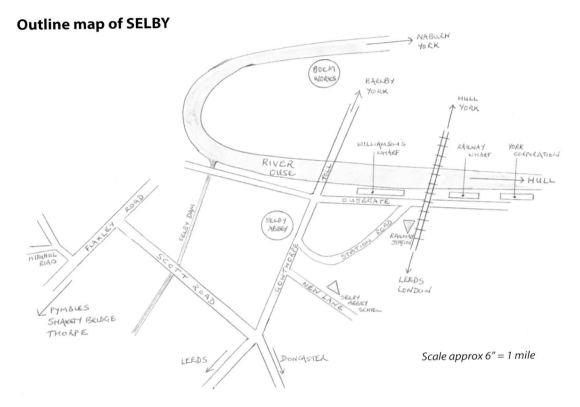

Scale approx 6" = 1 mile

there was easy access to the delights of the open fields, woods and streams.

'We moved in to Mirkhill Road and had a wonderful time. We could look out over fields to Brayton Barff, play football and cricket in the cornfields and Mr Dujardin, the boss at OCO, had his big house, The Pymbles, there. He was an aviator and used to fly his plane over the area, which we thought was great! He used to take off and land from Sherburn airfield just a few miles from Selby – and I'm sure when he flew over the cornfields, if we waved at him, he'd tip his wings and wave back at us.'

Brayton Barff, *barff* being from the Norse for 'small hill', is a wooded hillock in the village of Brayton, a couple of miles to the south of Selby. Climbing through the woods to the top gives a view back across the plain that Selby is situated on. As well as playing around the Barff, there were more attractions in the village of Thorpe Willoughby, that lay just beyond. In the

Map of parts of Selby that were important to Laurie when growing up. (Author)

summertime Laurie and his mates used to go out to play by Selby Dam, a tidal stream that runs from Thorpe Willoughby into the River Ouse in the centre of town.

'Mam would always warn us not to go swimming in the Dam, and we'd always promise not to – but when we got to our favourite spot, a little plank over the river we called Shakety (shaky) Bridge it'd be clothes off, straight in, diving and larking about. That's where we learnt to swim.

'Course we then had to spend a bit of time drying off and getting our hair straight – so when we got home and Mam said, "You've not been swimming at Shakety Bridge have you?" we could look her straight in the eye and say, "No Mam!" Sometimes you have to fib a bit.'

Mind you, sometimes not obeying authority could cause problems.

'When I was about thirteen I'd got a bike and would cycle around town with my mate David Sykes. One day we were cycling back home and there was a policeman on point duty at Scott Road. As we came towards him, he put his hand up telling us to stop, but lads being lads we cycled straight past. We didn't think he'd do anything but he chased us, caught us up and took our names and addresses. I was really worried and asked Dave what would happen. Dave reassured me – "Don't worry, he's just trying to scare us – he'll rip that bit of paper up when we're round the corner." I thought nothing more of it until next week – when Plop! – through the letterbox came a summons from the police. Mam was really annoyed. "You've let the family down what with your granddad being a policeman. You'll get a criminal record." We all had to go down to the Magistrates Court – stand in the pulpit with the brass rail and everything. We got fined five shillings. Quite a lot of money back then. Mrs Sykes was really unhappy. She searched in her purse and then threw the coins at the officer saying, "Here you are then – go off and buy yourself a new police helmet."'

Five shillings was quite a stiff fine – a fair portion of Sam's weekly wage. Laurie's bike could also be used to go on outings a bit further away from Selby.

'Sometimes of a Sunday afternoon we'd cycle the seven miles or so from Selby out to the lock at Naburn, just south of York. A quick shimmy down to the river bank and a quick change into cossies – and there you had it; a fine river for swimming in. The standard trick was to get in and swim the fifty yards across to the west bank and return.

Naburn Lock from the South, 1930 - just the era when Laurie and his mates would go swimming at the site.
(www.naburnvillage.org)

Any approaching craft had to sound their horn on approaching the lock, so there was no danger of being "run over".'

As well as individual outings, Laurie was in the local Scouts and played a cornet in the Scout Band. Canon Solloway at Selby Abbey used to lead the practice.

'When I played a bugle in the Scout Band, one of the highlights was the Sunday School outing to Bridlington. The families would meet

Selby Scout Band outside Selby Abbey in the early 1930s, lined up and ready to march under the leadership of Canon Solloway of Selby Abbey. (Laurie Dews)

Locomotive for children's seaside excursion at the north end of Selby station, with scout band in attendance.
(Author)

up in the middle of town and we'd meet up as a band too. We'd start playing and march in procession to Selby station. The big steam train would be waiting and we'd all pile on and put our instruments in the guard's van. When we got to Brid, we'd form up again and march them all down to the beach. Plenty of time for fun on the beach, a nice bite of afternoon tea in a cafe in town and then when it was home time we'd get together as a band and play some more tunes. That got everyone's attention so they formed up behind us again as we marched everyone back to Brid station for the return trip.'

Trips to the seaside were more for paddling and sandcastle creation than swimming in the sea. Swimming in a more formal way sometimes caused problems.

'I remember when we were going to swim in a competition at Selby Baths in the Park. I didn't have a swimming costume so Mam knitted me one – out of wool! When I got in and they got wet they dragged me down. I managed to do my length but when I got out at the end they were sagging right down to my knees!'

Outings like the one to Brid were fine, but Laurie could go on a special kind of jaunt all of his own – on Sam's barge down to Hull.

'But best of all was when the school summer holidays came round. Mam would pack some clothes in a case and bake some bread and cakes. This would all go in Dad's big basket, she'd lock the house and we'd all walk off early of a morning to the Railway Jetty in Ousegate. This jetty was opposite the old railway station. We would all go and live on board Dad's barge, the Selby Taurus. It was a marvellous feeling when we stepped on board at the Railway Jetty. Mother went down in the cabin to tidy things up and put the food in the cupboard, whilst me and my brother Frank stood on the cabin deck watching all the activity that was going on all around us. Men were shouting orders out and others were getting the tow ropes ready for when the tug came to tow us downriver to Hull.

'As well as the Taurus, there were usually three more barges to be on the tow, the Orion, Jupiter and Leo. The tug was the Robie, a steam tug with a big black and white funnel that had thick black smoke pouring out. When it arrived, the mate attached one tow rope from a barge to the port hook, and another to the starboard. The other two barges would hang their ropes onto the aft of the leading barges. It was now time for the journey to begin.

'When the tow ropes were put on the tug's towing hook, the captain gave a short blast on the tug's buzzer and my father let go of the stern rope which was hung on the jetty and we were on our way downstream to Hull. More smoke came out of the tug's funnel as the skipper rang the telegraph asking the engineer for more steam.

'When we were underway, Dad would steer with the tiller, and his mate would stow the ropes. Navigation had to be careful, as there were often half-built boats at Cochrane's shipyard on our starboard side and freighters unloading sugar beet or molasses at the sugar factory jetty on our port bow. After we had passed the shipyard and sugar factory

Profile of a Selby dumb barge.

(Alice Prince)

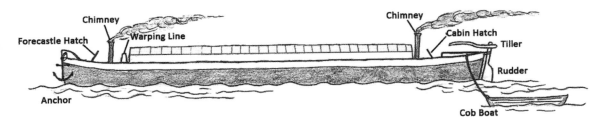

Cartoon by an
unknown artist of
a family in a
barge cabin.

*my father handed the tiller over to his mate who had just walked aft,
after securing the ropes on the forecastle. The mate's cabin was at the
fore end of the barge.*

*'We went down in the cabin where Mother had got our breakfast ready.
The cabin was a wonderful place. The door panels were all pine with
beautiful grain marking and the locker tops where we sat were all
mahogany and highly polished. The transom cupboards were mahogany
with two mirrors and all the knobs on the doors were brass. The cabin fire*

had a side oven which was black-leaded with brass knobs and a brass fender in front. The blower piece at the top would slide up and down to draw the fire up. Wooden steps with brass plates led up into the hatchway. The cabin floor always had a nice pegged rug on.

'We sat round the cabin table on the polished mahogany seats. Mam and Dad sat at the starboard side of the cabin table and Frank and me, we sat at the port side. That was called the "spare side". Over our heads swinging from the deck head was a brass paraffin lamp, which was the only light we had. Toilet facilities were primitive – either use a bucket or do it over the side!

It was said that if you found an un-identified body in the river you could tell if it was a bargeman – he'd have a bucket-shaped ring around his backside!

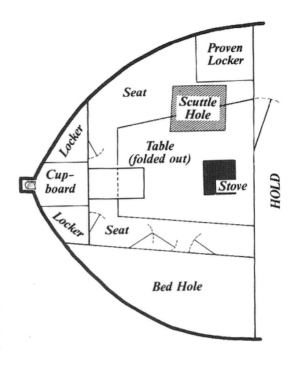

Diagram of layout of a barge cabin.

'Frank and I were soon back on deck to see what was going on. We could see and hear the water rushing by. It took us six hours to go from Selby to Hull. When we arrived in Hull and got moored up, all the Hull men went home.

'After getting moored up, it had come round to late afternoon, so Mam made tea and Dad rigged a sail up in the cob boat. My brother and I sailed all round the dock having a wonderful time. We also did a lot of fishing and if we caught flat fish, Mother would fry them for our teas, but if we caught any eels we would throw them back. They made a right mess of our lines with all their slime. Sometimes if we went into King George Dock there would be a Blue Funnel ship in, discharging bananas. They were still green needing time to ripen. Of course, if any fell in the water, we'd collect them and put them in a dark cupboard in the Taurus' cabin to do just that.

'There were numerous barges moored all round us in the dock, many with their families living on board, and on the warm summer evenings the bargemen used to sit round the cabin deck smoking their pipes and cigarettes, many of them "roll their own", supping a mug of sweet tea, telling stories of their voyages up and down the river, and singing music hall songs of the day.'

Some of these songs are described in Appendix 2. Sam may have had to censor one or two lines for the sake of the young lads' ears. Another thing that youths had to watch out for was the 'kid catcher'. The school truancy inspector would often do his rounds in and amongst the barges, and any under-fourteen-year-old could be dragged off, possibly literally, from the barge back to the classroom. Not so much fun for them, and one less hand to help on board.

'Hull Docks serviced not only the shipping along the Ouse, but also the trade up the Trent. The barges that used to go up to Gainsborough belonged to Farley's, who had a flour mill there. Those which went further up the Trent to Newark and Nottingham belonged to the Trent Navigation Co. who had a powerful tug, the Frank Rayner, *which towed the barges all the way from Hull to Nottingham.*

Common cargoes were grain for the flour mills and timber for construction. There was also traffic on the canals and waterways of South Yorkshire by connecting into the rivers Aire and Don around Goole.

'Many different barges used to go through the locks at Keadby on their way to Thorne with wheat, and some of the bargemen's names which come to my mind were the Carters, Deans and Blacknells.'

With all these bargemen meeting up for a chinwag over a cuppa, there was clearly a good chance of spreading news and gossip about the waterways. On summer nights, and possibly around the time of Hull Fair in October too, light-hearted bargemen's sports such as the greasy pole challenge might be organised.

In this a well-greased wooden pole was stretched some thirty feet or so from the dock-wall over the harbour. A flag was fixed to the far end, and the challenge was clear. Take a good run at it, sprint along the pole, grab the flag and you're 'cock of the walk'; sometimes there was a small prize. Of course, this was much more difficult than it sounds, and many a lad got a soaking in the docks – but eventually someone would make a despairing dive and snaffle the flag. That was usually a sign for a bit of rejoicing and drinks all round. Other sports events included women's sculling races, where wives and daughters would scull the cob boat around a course, sea-horse races, where a 'horse' would be made from an empty barrel and some planks and rowed around a course and swimming races across the width of the dock and back.

'At night when it was dark we sat in the cabin and the only light we had was the brass oil lamp hung in the middle of the cabin and as the ship rolled, so the lamp would swing backwards and forwards. I used to love that hypnotic rhythm.

'When it was time to go to bed, it was a quick wash in an enamel bowl filled with a dipper and a jug from the tank on deck. We slept in the spare side of the cabin and Mother and Dad slept in the "bed hole" as it was called, which was on the starboard side. There were two doors that folded back to let you in. It was like sleeping in a large cupboard that had tongue and groove boarding with a skylight over your head for illumination.

'When we woke up in the morning, light was streaming in through the skylights in the deckhead, and coming down the cabin hatch, the lovely smell of bacon being fried on the cabin stove. If the cargo holds were empty, Frank and I could go down and have a kick about or play cricket in the empty space using a rolled up sack or paper as a ball, or just run around. It was a huge space to play in.

'Dad would go to Whittaker's office on Alexandra Dock to get his orders as to where we had to load.'

Whittaker's were shipping agents in Hull. Whether you were working for a company or as a by-trader, independent of the major firms, the shipping agent was the point of contact between ships that had to be unloaded and lighters or barges that were available to do that unloading.

'When we were loaded and moving back up river, Frank and I sat behind the weatherboard, which was like a little wooden windbreak and kept the spray off us.

'Once we'd got back to Selby and moored up, Mother would pack up our clothes and we would all walk home to 1, Mirkhill Road. It did feel strange being home after being on board for ages, as the round trip was at least six days. You'd have one day going down to Hull, the next three days you'd be finding out what your load was and getting the cargo from the big ships, then you'd have to wait for the tide and the tug back up river. Sleeping at bedtime was the strangest, being in a proper bed and not hearing the water lapping outside. nor seeing the oil lamp's hypnotic sway.

'When I left school at fourteen, I got a job as an errand boy at the Co-operative on Flaxley Road. I stuck it for a year, but had some bad times with the manager. Although I worked from 8.30 in the morning till 6 at night, all for nine bob a week, one day he asked me to come in on a Sunday for some extra work as it was stocktaking time – but he said he'd see me right. So, as promised, I turned up at 8am and worked a straight five hours. Then at lunchtime came the bonus – a box of chocolates!

'That was enough for me so in 1937 I decided to go mate with my Dad on the Taurus, something I'd always wanted to do. I packed my bags, bought some sea boots, Mam knitted me a proper jersey and I got myself a cap and I walked through town to the Railway Jetty. I got to the Taurus and jumped aboard. At last I'd got the job I'd always wanted, I thought. We were away down the river to Hull and that was the start of my life as a boatman.

'I used to go mate on other barges too, to get a bit of extra cash. I remember being with one old keelman and his wife, and after I'd been steering for a bit he told me to go down into the cabin for some grub. Well his wife put some pork and spuds on my plate – and then poured the potato water over it as if it were gravy. Being a young lad I didn't mind a bit and I ate the lot.

'My father taught me how to become a bargeman. He showed me how to splice ropes and wires, and how to make fancy ships' fenders, the knotted ropes that protect the side of a boat from collisions. I learnt how to paint and how to do graining. That was where you made a piece of wood look like it had the grain showing. You had to paint it with some burnt umber first, then some red ochre and yellow ochre on top and draw a brush across it before it all dried. It was quite a skill. I made many friends in Hull, especially Harold Wray and Ted Taylor, who were mates like me on their father's ships, the Selby Capella and Leeds Jupiter.

The river journeys could give rise to incidents that gave a man a nickname for life. One such incident happened one foggy night.

'One time it had come in thick fog at South Ferriby so we had to ride at anchor. Someone suggested we should go ashore in the cob boat and have a drink in the village pub. So a few of us sculled the cob boat and tied up inside South Ferriby sluice and went to the pub. Me being a lad I only had a half but the others had a drink or two. When we all sculled back we decided it would be a good idea to make a pan of stew. Everyone got their tinned stuff open and put it in the pan, and it was all boiling away nicely when Ted Taylor said he'd got a tin of herrings. We all thought it would be a good idea to put those in too. Can't *remember what the stew tasted like, but he was always called "Herring" Taylor after that!*

'When the Taurus was laid over in Hull Docks for the weekend, Dad would go home on the train, but I'd stay on board and go round Hull with my mates, sometimes staying at Harold Wray's house in Victor Street, and at other times staying on board the Taurus, laid up at Alexandra Dock.'

Victor Street was in the Holderness Road part of Hull, and had a reputation, as Laurie put it, of being a 'bit of a rum area'. Whilst Sam was safely back in Selby, Laurie was getting a different kind of education with some of his mates out and about in Hull.

'There was a cafe just off the King George Docks called the Klondike and lots of the sailor lads would go in there. The owner had a big bull whip hung on the wall behind the counter. Any sign of trouble and he'd get it off the wall and literally crack the whip. Any trouble was soon settled!'

Laurie also encountered a different form of so-called 'trouble' when out with his barge mates.

Laurie as a teenager at Scarborough in 1938. (Laurie Dews)

'There were some right places around Alexandra Dock. One night the lads said, "Come out with us, you'll enjoy it." So they took me to the Bell, the King Billy then we ended up at this place called the Society Tavern. We all sat down in the best room and obviously the lads had set me up 'cos this bloke came into the room, eyed me up and down and said in a camp voice, "Well, I've never seen you before," sat down next to me and started putting his arm around me. Well ... I'd never seen anything like it before.'

The Society Tavern building still exists today, but it has been converted to flats. The King Billy and the Blue Bell remain licensed premises close to the former docks area.

Chapter 6

PICKING UP CARGO IN HULL DOCKS

Diagram of method of entry to Alexandra Dock. (Alice Prince)

Working barges and tug boats around Hull Docks was a time-consuming and complicated business, requiring plenty of skill and strength. Everything was subservient to the state of the tide. The Humber has a very large tidal range, and entrance to the docks depended on the depth of water. If you missed the tide when the river water was at the right height to enter the lock, you had to anchor up and ride out the tide until the river was at the required level again. Many of the BOCM crews lived in Hull, in which case they used their bikes, kept on board, to cycle home once their craft was securely tied up. Laurie and Sam were based in Selby, so missing the tide meant a wait of up to twelve hours. Laurie describes the procedure needed.

'Firstly, we had to get into Alexandra Dock, from the River Humber, where the cargo ships were ready to be unloaded. This required going through the lock. The tug Robie *left all the barges outside the dock where all the tow ropes were knocked off and the barges moored up against the jetty.* Robie *then returned to Hull Corporation Pier to tie up until the morning ready to tow loaded barges back up to Selby.*

'Meanwhile, the barge crew had to get into the lock to access the Dock and the cargo boats that were moored there. One of the mates would climb up the jetty (no ladders!) to ask the gatemen if they would let us in. A

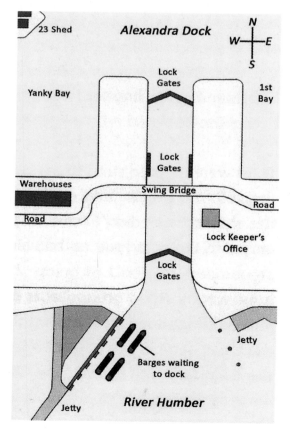

23 Shed

Alexandra Dock

N

W———E

S

Lock Gates

Yanky Bay

1st Bay

Lock Gates

Warehouses

Swing Bridge

Road

Road

Lock Keeper's Office

Lock Gates

Jetty

Barges waiting to dock

River Humber

Jetty

bit of banter and barter normally went on, and the going rate was about 2/- from each boat for the gateman to let us in. That was called penning money and is more like a fiver nowadays. Of course, the barges weren't powered, so it was only muscle power that could move the craft. There were two ways to do this, boat hooks or warping lines.

'My boat hook was a long pole of about twenty-four foot [6m] with a spike and a hook called a 'grain' on one end and a padded round piece of wood called a pummel on the other end which you placed against your shoulder to push the barge along.

'If it was very windy, we would use a warping line to winch the barge along, by one of us getting into the cob boat and sculling across the dock with one end of the line and securing it to the ship we were going to load from. Then you would signal to your mate and he would start winding the handle on the winch and as the line was wound in by hand, the barge would start moving across the dock.

'Ships were moored stern to the dock so that there could be barges to unload cargo into on both sides of the vessel. Another advantage to this was that the ship owners didn't have to pay wharfage costs as they

A Wren using a boathook, showing the way it could be used to propel an unpowered craft.

were at right angles to the wharf rather than alongside it, and a further saving was in using their own kit not the wharf cranes to unload.'

Wharfage was a charge made on ships when they were tied up in port. It could be levied against the tonnage of the ship, the length of time the ship occupied a berth and the length of dockside that the vessel covered. It was clearly in the ship owner's interest to moor up at right angles to the dock to reduce the third of these charges. The daily rate payable was another incentive for vessels to be unloaded as rapidly as possible.

'If we were loading ground nuts or palm kernels in sacks, it would take about a day and a half to load 225 tons. This was heaved out of the ships hold with the ships derrick, five bags at a time in a rope strop,

with all the mouths of the bags facing the same way. When they landed on the ship's deck, they were picked up again, dropped on a staging on the side of the ship where they were ripped and tipped down wooden chutes into the barge's hold. The emptied sacks weren't wasted. Once the contents had been tipped out, dockers would stack them in piles of twenty-five and throw them into the barge hatches. Once back at Selby, they'd be taken to the Bag House where women would wash them, repair any holes and return them to the factory for bagging the left-over 'meal' after the seed had been crushed for its oil.

'Blokes'd stand at the end of the gangway and the foreman would look 'em up and down. Then he'd go along the line and say, "I'll have you ... and you ... .and you" and so on until he'd got as many men as he needed, and if you weren't picked that was it for that ship. Some blokes would find out which pub the foreman drank in and 'leave a pint behind the bar' for the foreman hoping that would get them some work the next day.

'If the load was rice meal, the bags weren't split but had to be lowered into the hold by a derrick and the captain and his mate helped to stow the cargo assisted by two dockers. If the load was copra, cottonseed or locust beans, owners would put extra hatches on the side of the combings to increase the volume of the hold to allow more cargo in, as these materials "weighed light". Whatever the cargo, the covers had to be pulled over the hatches and wedges knocked in to keep them fixed. If the weather was bad, towing upriver meant that waves would wash right over the hatches as there were only a couple of inches of freeboard, that is how much the barge was above water level. So the covers were needed to keep the cargo dry.

'When we were fully loaded, we were given our orders to go to Selby, and told which tug was doing the towing. The lock was now hugely busy, as the lock gatemen opened the top gates and all the bargeman heaved and pushed their barges into the pound by boathook and warping line, to get the barges into position in the pen.'

The state of the river was again crucial. The tide that rushes in from the North Sea past Hull carries itself a long way inland along both the Ouse and Trent. As far as the Ouse is concerned, the incoming flood tide reaches as far as Naburn, several miles above Selby, can travel at anything up to eight knots and, at the extreme Spring tides can produce a considerable difference in depth of water in the river. To harness such a force of nature

OPPOSITE: Cargo being unloaded into barges by a variety of methods in Hull Docks in the 1950s. Loose seed is being tipped from a ripped-open sack down a chute into the left-hand barge. The large towing ropes can be seen coiled in the foreground, and the smaller warping line is wrapped around a roller. The barge on the immediate right is receiving full sacks into its hold, whilst more tipping is going on further along the deck.

(Waterways World)

clearly makes for a more efficient journey upstream, so the tug and its barges planned to travel with the tide. The moment when the tide started flowing is called tide time and runs for around five hours at Hull. Irrespective of time of the day or night, bargemen and tug skippers had to be ready to take advantage of the flow.

Awaiting the tide, barges were penned up together to allow the tug to gather up her craft for the journey to Selby. The trip to Selby normally consisted of four loaded barges, towed in pairs. Mates on the two barges that were going to be at the front of the squadron passed 100 feet (30m) of rope to the barges that were to be in the rear, ready for the journey. These ropes were sturdy, usually 10in (25 cm) diameter, made of natural hemp, and possibly wet through. Quite a weight!

Next, the tug came astern into the lock and the mate threw a 120ft (35m) heaving line to be made fast on each of the barges which were to be nearest the tug. There was one towing line from each of the tug's hooks – one on the starboard side, one on the port. Tug and barges were now ready. As many as twenty barges with their associated tugs could be nosing their way around the lock with cargoes for Gainsborough, Nottingham, and Lincoln via the Trent, Leeds via the Ouse and Aire, and Goole and York via the Ouse as well as Selby itself. Coal fumes from the cookers on the barges melded with steam from the tug's funnel and the odours from oil or coal-fired boilers on the tugs made for a heady and never-to-be-forgotten aroma signalling departure from Hull.

The next action was allowing the flotilla out into the river. The lock gateman closed the top gates, blew a whistle and then opened the cloughs in the lock gates, causing the water level in the lock to fall until it was the same level as the water in the river. The lock gates then opened. For barges going upstream, which most of them were, these gates were opened after the flood had been flowing for an hour or so, four hours before high water at Hull. *Robie* began to pull her fleet and when the rope on the leading barges pulled tight, then barges in the rear had their 100ft (30m) of rope called into action.

'When all these tow ropes were taut, a cry of "All tight!" came from each barge. Robie's skipper rang the telegraph for full steam ahead and down below the stoker shovelled coal to deliver the power.'

The barges, bearing a frosted paraffin lamp on the forecastle, and those in the rear another glowing dully red on their stern rails, headed off into the shipping channels of the often dark and foreboding River Humber. For barges carrying a liquid cargo, turning upstream was a hazardous moment. This manoeuvre placed the cargo temporarily broadside to the swell on the Humber. Once the tow was under way, a good trip would take about six hours all told. But that wasn't six hours of rest and relaxation. Whatever the weather, at least one man had to be at the tiller keeping the barges apart and out of the tug's backwater, whilst not allowing them to drift too far apart. Sometimes cross-ropes helped with this aspect. Generally, steering was done by a wooden tiller, a mighty piece of timber, with enough force behind it to push Sam Dews overboard! But it wasn't just the direction of travel you had to watch out for. Skippers were paid by the weight of cargo carried, so the barges were filled until there was as little as 6in (15 cm) of freeboard.

Barges ready to leave Hull Docks. This image gives some idea of how busy and congested the dock area could become when it was time for the barges to go onto the river.
(Yorkshire Waterways Museum)

A Whitaker's barge at Selby, riding very low in the water, showing the extent to which the freeboard of a barge could be reduced. (Author)

If you had to walk the length of the barge, more than likely you had to do it on a surface made slimy by the wash of river water, with the ever-present danger of slipping overboard. Furthermore, the barges were travelling at quite a pace. If you want to have steerage on a river, you have to be moving faster than the tide – otherwise you're nothing more than a big stick. If the tide is running at six knots, when observed from the bank you have to have a speed greater than that.

Leaving aside those requirements, every now and then a big cloud of sulphurous smoke came out of the tug's funnel as the stoker chucked some more coal on the fire to keep a full head of steam.

Then, of course, there was the weather. On a pleasant summer's day, it could easily be an enjoyable cruise. But the barge traffic was a year-round operation, and the Humber often experienced poor conditions. In cold weather, the spray from the river froze on the tow rope.

'If the cold brought snow, on a winter's day going upstream into the teeth of a gale or a howling blizzard there was no protection for the man at the tiller. We did about one-hour spells on the tiller wrapped

in our big top coats and balaclava helmets to keep our ears warm.
Under these conditions, after that hour you could end up looking like
a snowman! A tot of rum from the cabin store helped you to warm back
up. What a lovely feeling it was when your mate came to spell you and
you could go down to the lovely warm cabin with a nice open coal fire
glowing and the brass paraffin lamp glowing. I don't think lads these
days would put up with such conditions.'

Then again, there was the opposite to wind and snow; fog, in
many ways the most dangerous of all. You had to have total
trust in the tug skipper and his crew keeping a keen look out.
You had to have the confidence that the tug was pulling you
along the correct channel, and that a string of barges was not
coming downstream towards you. As Sam's log shows, there
were plenty of places where you could moor up and wait for
conditions to improve, but time was money. You didn't get paid
until your load had been delivered. Should you moor up and
be safe, but miss the tide and be delayed by twelve hours? Or
should you be brave and push on and get paid a day earlier?

Having mastered the skills of steering the barges, and being
prepared for the vagaries of the weather, there were yet more
skills to learn. The convoy had to navigate across and around
shallows, through the turbulence created by bridge pillars and
finally the complex unloading arrangements at Selby.

Laurie started his barge career in 1937, and in the normal run
of things would have been expected to serve out an
'apprenticeship' learning those skills over the course of the next
few years. Unfortunately, that process was interrupted by
another situation where a bargeman's skill and strength was
needed; the Second World War.

Chapter 7

WARTIME EXPERIENCES

In 1940, Hull was, and remains now, one of the UK's major ports, and as such a key site for the import and export of goods. The barge fleet extended that transport artery for many miles inland. In wartime, this made the city, the docks and associated waterways a major target for enemy attack in the Second World War. Geography made any attack a relatively simple task; on returning from sorties over the industrial heartlands of the West Riding, it was straightforward to follow the course of the rivers to Hull, where any bombs not dropped on Sheffield or Leeds could effectively be discharged. Between 1940 and 1945, Hull became the most severely damaged British city, with over 85,000 buildings, including ninety-five per cent of houses, damaged or destroyed. Of a population of approximately 320,000 at the beginning of the war, about half were made homeless. Much of the city centre was completely destroyed and heavy damage was inflicted on residential areas, industry, the railways and the docks. Despite the damage and heavy casualties, the port continued to function throughout the war. This vast destruction was not widely known, as broadcasters referred, for tactical reasons, to a 'north-east coast town' rather than name the city itself.

Of course, commerce had to continue, so the barges kept plying their trade.

'Not long after the war had started one night we were moored up in Hull and Harold Wray and I had been out for a drink. We kipped in his attic, and although we might have had a few pints, we were certain that Harold's attic had had a roof when we went out. In the morning it seemed a bit bright and breezy; it turned out we'd slept through an air raid and Harold's roof had lost a few tiles so that we could see broad daylight!

'On another cold winter's night in 1940, I was asleep on my own on board Taurus *when I was woken by the sound of someone shouting out. I jumped out of bed, pulled a jersey and boots on, went up on deck and I could hear a bloke in the water of the dock, shouting for help. I slid down a rope into the cob boat and sculled across the dock. I got to*

the man who was making the racket, and when I got within reach he gripped the boat and wasn't going to let go! I pulled him on board – and it was clear that he wasn't English. I got him to the dock side where a policeman and air raid warden were waiting, and got him onto the quay. I sculled quietly back to the Taurus *and got back in my bunk. "A good job done", I thought. I guessed he was a German aviator who had parachuted out of a stricken plane and landed in the Docks, but never heard any more about it.'*

From the summer of 1940, raids on Hull became an almost weekly event. Twenty-one separate raids are listed as affecting the city between June and December 1940. Bargemen had a difficult choice to make; stay with your barge, hope to pick up more cargo, and so more pay, but with the danger of being in a wooden barge when incendiary bombs were being dropped. Hull-based men could take refuge by cycling home, but Sam and Laurie needed a return train to Selby, leaving the barge untended and not being in a position to earn money for a week or so. A tough choice.

'After one raid in May 1941, Dad said he'd had enough and was off on the train home. I decided to stay, with my mate Johnny Roddam on the Selby Pollux. *When the bombers came on the first night we managed to put out any fires with sandbags. Just after 11pm the next night, they showered the dock with incendiary bombs and set warehouses and several barges on fire.'*

The heaviest raids of the war in Hull to date took place on the city on the nights of 7, 8 and 9 May 1941. The air raid warning was sounded just after 11pm on 7 May and stayed in force for six hours. The raids on the next night went on for a similar length of time. Thousands of incendiary bombs and a great weight of parachute mines and high explosive bombs were dropped. Whilst the attacks were mainly concentrated on the centre of the city and the docks, all areas in the city suffered damage. There were many serious fires, causing extensive damage to business, commercial and domestic property.

'The Taurus *was set alight. Johnny and I tried all night to put the fires out, but we couldn't, so we had to abandon her and get ashore. Many of the wooden barges began to sink as the fires began to burn their dry timbers. We could hardly breathe because of the*

*smoke. Even a rail locomotive was on fire as an incendiary had
landed in her coal bunker.*

'The Leeds Vulcan *was moored by 21 bay in Alexandra Dock
when a bomb exploded near the fo'c'sle blowing a hole in it, and the
barge shot away across the dock like a speedboat. Luckily, no-one was
on board.'*

The *Leeds Uranus* was moored outside Lime Street Dry Dock,
took a direct hit and was completely destroyed. They say that
pieces of the barge were found in the ruins of the nearby
bombed out Alexandra Theatre. Other barges were sunk and
yet others, including the *Taurus*, caught fire, but many were
eventually repaired at Brown's Dry Dock.

*'When they started dropping explosive bombs we had to dash into
an air raid shelter. Before we got there, we saw a big grey cylinder
floating down on a parachute that got caught on the jib of a crane.
Johnny and I managed to find a barge that hadn't been burnt out and
nipped into the cabin to make a brew. When we came out there were
these two soldiers taking out a fuse. Turned out we'd nearly been hit by
a parachute bomb and we'd known nowt about it. I managed to cut off
a piece of the parachute cord, and took it home and put it in the shed.'*

Laurie wasn't the only one to make use of this unexpected
supply of material. After all, there was a war on, meaning
shortages, with clothing rationing starting in June 1941, so the
chance of a bit of cotton or silk for a blouse from an enemy
parachute was not to be passed up lightly.

'When the air raid was over, we walked back to the Taurus *and she
was a smouldering wreck. We had lost everything. It was no use
hanging around so we went off to the station to get a train home. Lots
of people thought we had been killed. When we walked off the dock the
police and wardens wondered where we had come from, as they
wouldn't let anyone onto the dock because of unexploded bombs.*

*'The walk back to Hull Paragon station was a bit of a struggle over
the debris from bombed buildings. All the wooden setts in the street
were raised up and there were pools of water from the fire hoses. When
me and Johnny finally got home to Selby, Mother thought we must
have been killed as they'd been able to see the flames and bombs
exploding, forty miles away in Selby. She played hell with Dad. "Why
didn't you make him come home with you?"'*

BOCM mill in Hull ablaze next to the River Hull.

(Hull Remembers)

Many factories and mills on the river Hull were either gutted by fire or destroyed by high explosives. Rank's Flour Mills, one of the biggest flour mills in the country, was devastated. Considerable damage was done to the docks and buildings on both sides of the Old Harbour were destroyed by fire and high explosives The raids left 400 dead and 758 injured.

Dad couldn't believe that the Taurus was burnt out. Whilst he was without a barge, he went to work in the BOCM stores in Selby and I went mate with Guy Dyson on my dad's old barge, the Selby Vega *but after one unsuccessful trip I left him, because he was tight with his money, and I went to work on other barges.*

Barrage balloons were one passive way that the city could be protected from aerial attack. Initially based at sites on land, the balloons were filled with highly-flammable hydrogen gas. The defence was not so much the balloons themselves, but various explosive devices that were attached to the wires that linked the balloon to the ground. The combination of explosive gas and explosive devices was extremely hazardous. Floating balloon sites using commandeered barges, moored to buoys at appropriate positions on the river were rapidly developed to protect the Humber Dock area. These creations were known as the 'Waterborne' and were crewed by RAF staff. Later on,

Firefighters at work
on the River Hull.
(Hull Remembers)

barrage balloons were attached to fishing or coasting craft that
the forces had taken over. These craft would move along the
river in an attempt to stop enemy planes laying mines in the
Humber. This fleet became known as 'His Majesty's Drifters'.

During the war, many of the barges were commandeered by
the military and were fitted with a barrage balloon and moored
in the middle of the River Humber to stop enemy aircraft
bombing the docks.

Barrage balloon
over Hull Docks.
(Hull Remembers)

'One day my mate Freddie Holdgate arrived in Hull with his barge
Selby Sirius empty. Some military types came over to have a word.
They said they needed his barge for military
service and they were going to take it right
away. Freddie didn't have any choice in the
matter. Just a few minutes to get all his
belongings together and clear out. Three other
of our barges were taken like that to use as
mooring posts for barrage balloons.

'One barge was moored outside Alexandra
Dock waiting for the morning tide and during
the night enemy planes came over and
dropped some motion mines in the river. Next
morning when the mate started the engine up,
everything was blown to pieces. Another

coaster coming upriver from Hull forgot to wind in his balloon and fouled power cables at Whitgift, meaning that the balloon caught the cables and burst into flames.

'Many of the bargemen like myself volunteered to join the forces. Some manned landing craft and others were on Rescue Tugs. I was on the landing craft when I went into the Special Combined Operations in 1942 and took part in the D-Day landings.'

When barge crews had been called up, a bargeman's wife might have to crew a trip. As bargees didn't want to let on, rather than admit to having the wife as crew, there might be a coy reference to having a new 'long-haired mate'.

'After I'd joined up, my mother went with Dad on the repaired Taurus, *going up and down the river and helping to load the cargo. She told the tale of when they were loaded up with peanuts in King George Dock, and Dad had gone ashore for a couple of pints. Mother was sat in the cabin, knitting, when she heard a loud bump. Looking out of the hatchway, she saw a tug had come alongside and the crew were busy filling a bag with peanuts. Mother responded by telling the tug men, "You can have as many nuts as you like if you put plenty of your coal onto my cabin deck!"*

'Dad came back refreshed and when he saw the coal he thought he might have had too much, as he didn't know where all the coal – best Yorkshire Hards, mind you – had come from. Mother told him, and Sam thought it was a good deal.

The crew of the LBE 18: the landing craft that Laurie was on in the D Day landings at Arromanches. Laurie is 4th from the right on the bottom row. LBE stood for Landing Barge: Emergency repair. Amongst other duties, LBE 18 delivered a workshop lorry onto Gold Beach. All the crew survived after the craft beached during the gales of 19/22 June.

(Laurie Dews)

In wartime, coal was hard to come by, and the company didn't provide any. The captain had to buy it out of his wages, or, as money was short, obtain fuel without paying. The full bunkers of the sea-going steam tugs were a great temptation, especially as the cob boats were so nippy.

'I remember back in the winter of 1940, I was moored up in Hull Docks with my dad on Taurus *and all the barges were frozen together.*

Postcard from the front line, a few days after LBE 18 had been beached in June 1944. It's good to know that Laurie could tell his mam that he was 'quite well' after all he must have been through.

(Laurie Dews)

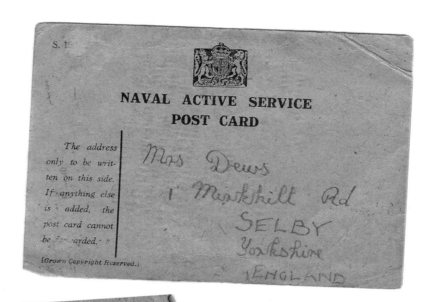

S. 1.

NAVAL ACTIVE SERVICE POST CARD

The address only to be written on this side. If anything else is added, the post card cannot be forwarded.

[Crown Copyright Reserved.]

Mrs Dews
1 Montkhill Rd
SELBY
Yorkshire
ENGLAND

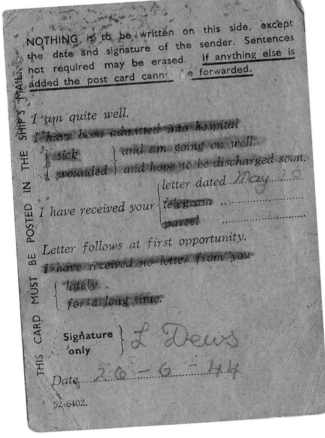

NOTHING is to be written on this side, except the date and signature of the sender. Sentences not required may be erased. If anything else is added the post card cann' e forwarded.

I am quite well.

I have been admitted into hospital
{ sick } and am going on well.
{ wounded } and hope to be discharged soon.
letter dated May 2 0
I have received your { telegram ....
{ parcel ....
Letter follows at first opportunity.
I have received no letter from you
{ lately .
{ for a long time.

Signature } L Dews
only

Date 26 - 6 - 44.

52-6402.

THIS CARD MUST BE POSTED IN THE SHIP'S MAIL.

We were getting low on coal so Johnny Roddam and another friend, Fred Shipley, got in the cob boat and moored it alongside one of the sea-going tugs whose bunkers were full. We put loads into our boat and sculled back to our barges. By, it was grand to see a nice big fire blasting out in our cabin.'

Although the barges weren't powered, you needed coal to keep the fire going for warmth and for cooking.

As for Laurie's actual D-Day experiences and wartime service – well there are some things that perhaps are best not recalled. Having completed service in the forces, Laurie returned home in 1946 to resume his career on the Ouse.

Chapter 8

NEW PARTNERS AT HOME AND AT WORK

The world on Civvy Street that Laurie returned to after the war was very different to the one he had left behind in 1942. There had been physical damage inflicted upon Hull and the Docks, and several of the barges had been badly damaged. When experienced skippers returned from the war, those that had remained behind to be in temporary charge of the vessels had to relinquish their control and return to more junior roles.

'When I returned after the war in 1946, I went skipper of the Selby Castor. *This was quite a step up – being in charge of my own barge at the age of twenty-four.'*

The *Castor* was another dumb barge but, unlike the *Vega*, was capable of carrying both liquid and solid cargoes. Laurie was also involved in a more personal change of role.

'When I was on leave from the Navy in 1942. I went to the Blackburn's of Brough dance at the Beverley Road baths with my mate Jim Hiley who was on the same landing craft as me. We went with his wife Lil and her sister Marian. That's where Marian and I first met.'

Courting whilst you were in the services was hard, only being able to meet up when you were on leave. One leave saw Laurie in Marian's bad books.

'One time I was on leave and I didn't get round to seeing Marian till the day before I was due back. I called round her house on Rose Street, knocked on the door, and her mam came out. She looked me up and down and said, "I don't think you're welcome here. You've not come round to see Marian and she's turned your picture on the mantelpiece to face the wall."'

That scrape got sorted out, but being young lads, Laurie and his mates naturally had an eye for a girl. Sadly, sometimes they

Laurie and Marian
Dews on their
wedding day,
28 December 1946.

(Laurie Dews)

mixed their beaux up with their barge. Both had curvaceous qualities, but trouble arose if they confused the two.

'Barges built at Thorne were a bit rounder in the rear than those built at Beverley. Sometimes we'd look at a lass and say to each other – "By, she's Thorne built." If a girlfriend who knew us heard us say something like that we'd get a sharp poke in the ribs.'

Happily, all went well with Laurie and Marian.

'I got demobbed in 1946, but I always say that pretty soon I joined up again 'cos I got married. Between Christmas 1946 and New Year 1947, on 28 December, Marian and I wed in Hull. The ceremony was at St Silas, but that's been demolished now. Our reception was above the Regal Cinema and the honeymoon was two days in Blackpool.'

Saint Silas was a companion of Saint Paul on his missionary journeys throughout the Middle East. In the gospels, he is often referred to as 'Silvanus'. The church was in Barmston Street, Sculcoates, about half a mile from the Docks.

'Marian was a "Hullie", and we worked a few trips together. We didn't have a place to call our own, so some of the time we stayed at Marian's parents in Hull, and sometimes with my parents in Selby. The barges were working non-stop, so I used to spend a lot of time away from home. Raymond, our eldest son, was born in 1947, but it wasn't until five years later in 1952 we finally got a new council house in Selby, down Petre Avenue.'

March 1947 brought some of the largest floods in living memory to the Ouse catchment. High water levels and strong currents made navigation almost impossible. The OCO factory at Barlby was flooded to a depth of several feet, and so its workings were

Soldiers rescuing inhabitants from Millgate, central Selby, following the flooding of March 1947. (Author)

Army DUKW vehicle moving along Barlby Road, with the Olympia Hotel in the background, in the wake of the Selby floods of March 1947. (Author)

WHEN BARLBY BANK BROKE

It was during Saturday night and Sunday morning that the Barlby bank broke, and thousands of gallons of water rushed through on to the York-Selby road, flooding it at depths varying from one to three feet, over a distance of two miles. Unchecked, the water raced on, washing away the ballast from the Selby-York and Selby-Hull railway lines. Services had to be suspended, and traffic to York was diverted by way of Church Fenton. The floods swept along, covering the Cooperage, the Sauce Factory, the O.C.O., and the Potato Factory grounds; and, because of the conditions, the sewage pump at Barlby could not be operated, thus adding to the difficulties.

A reporter was told, " We were powerless to deal with the position when the bank broke," and that the bank had shown signs of cracking in several other places. Gangs of workmen were busy with the aid of electric lights throughout Saturday-Sunday night, piling sand-bags at danger-points on the banks, principally near Third Estate and the Ardol jetty. The position would have been less serious had not urgent work on strengthening the banks been held up for two months on account of the heavy snow and frost. Piles of brushwood intended for this work were lying on top of the bank for the best part of a mile.

It was not until daylight that one could get a true picture of the severity of the position. Hardly a street from Selby toll-bridge to Barlby Senior School had escaped the ravages of the flood. Families marooned in their bedrooms, who had spent Saturday night barricading their doors, cooked alfresco meals over their small bedroom grates and spent the morning with their heads out of the windows as they anxiously watched the water rushing down the streets.

At O.C.O., the largest factory in the area, the water made its way into the works, and the conveyor-belt system at the bottom of the seed silos was put out of operation. When the floods invaded the grounds of the Cooperage, hundreds of barrels were floated, and some made their way on to the main York road. Where the water from the breach failed to reach, the Ouse, by overflowing opposite The Holmes and running down the streets in that locality, did the district a bad turn.

enshire and Goole Advertiser

SELBY'S SORRY STATE

THE WORST FLOODS IN LIVING MEMORY

ALL THE MAIN ROADS UNDER WATER

FARMERS SUFFER BADLY

BARLBY IN GREAT DANGER

ABOVE: *Selby Times* headline concerning flooding in Selby, March 1947. (Author)

LEFT: An extract from the *Selby Times* describing how the floods affected the area of the Barlby factory. (Author)

greatly reduced. Near Selby where the banks were breached, old barges were used to form the core of an emergency replacement bank.

'When Sam retired in 1953, I left the Castor *and took over my father's barge the* Taurus.'

Dumb barges were coming to the end of their useful working life of almost forty years; for instance, the *Castor* had been launched in 1915 and was still going strong in 1952, but shortly after OCO became BOCM in 1951, the company showed confidence in the future of river-borne transport by investing in a new fleet of motorized barges. By using motorized barges, the need for a tug was removed and also many of the skills needed in handling dumb barges were no longer needed. The new barges also brought a fresh degree of creature comfort, as well as increased safety and a reduced dependence on the state of the tides. Each barge had a new brass bell indicating its date of launch.

'In 1954 at the age of 32, I became skipper of the new motor barge Selby Corrie, *which could carry 200 tons, like the dumb barges.'*

BOCM's decision to make this investment in a fleet of commercial barges was the last of its kind in the UK. Richard Dunston of Thorne were contracted to build eighteen craft between 1953 and 1962. The cost of each vessel was about £15,000 (perhaps £300,000 today) but as the value of each full cargo load could easily top £1,000, the barges were good value. The *Corrie* might have been a new, motorized barge, but there was still plenty of old-fashioned hard work. The lighting was still by oil lamp, and before it got dark every night, the crew had to make sure all the lights were well fettled. The drill was: open up the light and clean the glass with newspaper; trim the wick to make it short and level so that there wasn't too yellow a flame that would smoke the glass; fill up with paraffin; light the wick and finally close down the glass.

The bell from the *Selby Tony*, one of the members of the BOCM fleet.

(York Artsbarge)

That had to be done for each of the navigation lights on the barge – the masthead, the port and starboard lamps and the stern chase – the light to the rear. Light was also needed in the cabin and also in the engine room. That's six lights in all – a good hour's work every night.

The later motorized barges were fitted with electric lights, which was a great boon. An hour of fiddly and smelly work banished, and strong, steady light at the flick of a switch. Sailing without lights was an offence however. When the lights fused on Laurie's barge when he was docking in 1980, a policeman spotted him, reported him to the authorities and a £50 fine ensued.

'If you had any problems cleaning out the engine filters that all had to be done by oil light, and what a fiddle that was. Just getting a match stalk in the filters could stop the Lister 60hp engine. And what a smell in the engine room to start it. Paraffin fumes from the lamp and the smell of commercial diesel as you had to pump up the compressor and swing the flywheel to start the engine up!'

Trade was very busy throughout the 1950s.

'We were running up and down the river day and night and the normal payload was to bring 200 tons of seed upriver from Hull and

Launch of the
Selby Michael at
Thorne, 1960.
(Laurie Dews)

take 150 tons of soya meal back to BOCM mill at Hull. The company continued to invest in their craft and in 1959 I went to Thorne to take charge of a new, more powerful motor barge, the Selby Martin *that carried 250 tons. Finally, in 1960, I went to Thorne again and took charge of yet another new barge, the* Selby Michael.

'I spent many happy hours' as skipper of the Michael. *As well as working the Ouse, we did a few trips up the River Trent running to Spillers' mill at Gainsborough with soya meal from Selby.'*

The era from the introduction of the motorized barges through-out the 1950s until the coming of motorways, heavy-duty lorries and containerization in the late 1970s could be seen as a golden era for barge traffic on the Ouse.

Chapter 9

THE JOURNEY UPRIVER FROM HULL

In a similar way that London cabbies have the 'Knowledge', a bargeman gained and applied his understanding of the river over a lifetime voyaging between Hull and Selby. Whether as mate, skipper of a dumb barge or a motorized one, as a bargeman learnt his trade he became familiar with the topography of the river. He came to know about the dangers of bends and shallows; sand banks and nesses; weather and tides. He recognized the importance of various buoys, riverbank features and landmarks. He gained an understanding of the tricks of the trade and of the tales of incidents and accidents that

Map of the river journey from Hull to Barton. (Alice Prince)

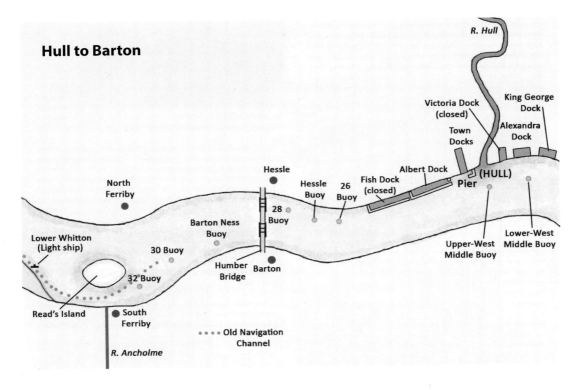

Hull to Barton

R. Hull

King George Dock

Victoria Dock (closed)

Town Docks

Alexandra Dock

Albert Dock

Hessle

North Ferriby

Hessle Buoy

26 Buoy

Fish Dock (closed)

(HULL)

Pier

Barton Ness Buoy

28 Buoy

Lower Whitton (Light ship)

30 Buoy

Humber Bridge

Barton

32 Buoy

Upper-West Middle Buoy

Lower-West Middle Buoy

Read's Island

South Ferriby

Old Navigation Channel

R. Ancholme

Diagram of the towing formation for OCO barges being pulled upstream.
(Alice Prince)

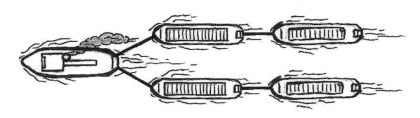

Towing formation

occurred along the way. The maps feature many of the places that Laurie mentions.

'Leaving Alexandra Dock, Hull, we navigated upstream, passing the Lower West Middle red light buoy on our port side and then Victoria Dock to starboard with all the ships riding at anchor, loaded with timber and pit props waiting to enter the dock to discharge.'

The convoy craft once in the river saw the tug with two barges on both port and starboard sides, as in this diagram.

'Then past Old Harbour and the River Hull with Sammy Point at the entrance where years ago there used to be a garrison. Moored at the double-decker pier would be the paddle steamer **Lincoln Castle**, one of a fleet of three that ferried passengers and cars across the river to New Holland in Lincolnshire. Sammy Point got its name from a chap who used to own a windlass there in the days when sailing ships needed assistance to get into Old Harbour.

'Flashing on our port side was Upper West Middle gas buoy, then past Albert Dock with its famous clock tower and Riverside Quay where ships moored alongside. Fruit-carrying ships unloaded here as well as the 'Abbey' ships that sailed regularly to Rotterdam.

'There were more vessels riding off Albert Dock such as trawlers loaded with fish waiting to pass into the Fish Dock, otherwise known as St Andrew's Dock. There was an "insurance marker" buoy here. These were buoys placed in potentially hazardous sites in an attempt to avoid accidents. Ships were warned not to anchor west of this as some trawlers had come to grief when they had done just that.'

One was the Hull trawler *Edgar Wallace* which had been involved in a widely reported tragedy on 9 January 1935. Fifteen lives were lost from a crew of eighteen when the vessel foundered. She was within sight of home when she foundered, having steamed nearly 1,400 miles with a cargo of fish from Bear Island in the Arctic. She arrived off the Fish Dock abreast of four or five other vessels but could not get clear of them, and bumped twice on the Hessle sand bar, making the vessel list to port. Water rushing in along with the movement of a full cargo of fish meant that she could not right herself. Many of those who died were trapped below decks. Two of the three survivors were picked up having clung onto the wireless mast before it snapped. In Laurie's early days, this part of the river was unremarkable but in 1972, construction of the mighty suspension bridge linking the northern and southern banks of the Humber near Hessle was begun. Some forty or so years in planning, the crossing opened in 1981. As Laurie regularly

LEFT: View taken from the River Ouse of the Humber bridge under construction.
(Laurie Dews)

RIGHT: View from the River Ouse of the Humber bridge under construction.
(Laurie Dews)

passed the construction site, he was able to take pictures of the work as it proceeded.

He was also able to marvel at the balancing skills of the workmen.

'Sometimes we'd look up at the lads working on the bridge – just seeming to walk along the suspension cables without a care in the world – or a safety net! They'd sometimes wave at us as we passed by on the river.'

Tacking across the river to find the navigation channel was a constant challenge.

'The next buoy was 26A, a red flashing buoy and after that came the light from Hessle. Passing Hessle, we headed across the river towards Barton Ness buoy to the south of Read's Island.'

Leaving aside any dredging that may have gone on, the position of the deep water channel depended on the tides and the time of year. Generally speaking, there were summer and winter channels. In a tidal river like the Humber or Ouse, in wintertime, the volume of water coming downstream on the ebb tide generally had more force than the inrushing flood caused by the tide. The situation would be reversed in summer. This would make no difference along a rack, but coming round a hoop or a bight, the favoured course would constantly alter. Those in charge of the river navigation monitored the situation regularly and changed the positions of buoys accordingly. A particular example occurred at Read's Island.

'Read's Island had just one house on and a few sheep. They say it was created by a galleon sinking there hundreds of years ago and the sand and silt built up all round it making the island as it is today.'

The 1734 Customs Map of the Humber shows a sandbank in the area called Old Warp. Villagers later sank a ship to allow silt to build up around the wreck to increase the size of the island and protect the riverbank around South Ferriby. Other sources describe it as being made of 'Pudding Pie Sand' and that it took its name from Mr Read of Burton Stather on the south bank. At Spring Tides, it was possible for cattle to walk across the island. Permanent residence ceased around 1989. The navigation channel is normally to the north of the island, but occasionally the conditions in the river create a navigable course in the narrow straight between the island and the south bank of the Humber.

'On the port side we pass South Ferriby with its sluice and Eastwood's cement works. Also at South Ferriby are a lock and the entrance to the River Ancholme. On we go past Wintringham Haven, passing Lower Whitton and across to Brough, passing Oyster Ness buoy. Passing Brough Aerodrome we can see the slipway where they used to launch the seaplanes and the black mooring buoy they used to moor to.'

Brough Aerodrome was originally owned by the Blackburn Aeroplane and Motor Company, and tested seaplanes during the First World War. Over the next half century or so, many designs of aircraft were built and tested here, until the firm ultimately became part of British Aerospace. During the 1950s, the perimeter track was used for motor racing, and Stirling Moss won one of his first races there.

'Passing on our port side is Middle Whitton light ship, followed by Upper Whitton light ship. Each of the Whitton ships were manned by two men one week on and a week off.'

A similar light ship to this – the one from Spurn – is now moored in Hull Marina.

Upper Whitton lightship (above) as in service in the 1950s and (lower) in Grimsby dock, 1997. There were three Whitton lightships: Upper, Middle and Lower. Two crew used to live aboard each. Laurie recalls that as it was a lonely job, if conditions were favourable, the bargemen would circle one of the ships and pass the men a Sunday newspaper to keep them occupied during quiet times.

(Laurie Dews)

'The Whitton Sands are very dangerous sands, similar to the Goodwin Sands in the English Channel. If a boat grounded on them when the tide was ebbing, the sand would whittle away from underneath the ship and if she was loaded, might break her back. Many craft have come to grief on Whitton Sands. The Lower lightship was by far the hardest to work on. A whirlpool effect caused by the tides was so strong there that the vessel was constantly being pulled in different directions on its anchor, meaning little rest for the crew.'

One such sloop was the *Masterman* which turned over on Whitton Sands. As Laurie remembers it, the story had a happy ending.

'The captain's wife and two children were locked in the cabin and when they cut a hole in the barge, they found the woman alive, holding the baby in her arms. She had been in an air pocket.'

However, according to local newspaper reports, the outcome was somewhat more unfortunate and the Whitton village website has the full detail:

'On the morning of the 26 June 1906 the sight of a wreck, the sloop Masterman, presented itself close to the foreshore, embedded in Whitton Sand. A telegram was sent to Brough and it was learned that the crew had managed to escape and had landed there, but that five women had been trapped below, in the cabin and had drowned. They were Mary Ann Barr (46) of Hull and her four daughters Emily Eastwood (20), Frances Barr (15), Jane Barr (9) and Joy Barr (7). The bodies were never recovered but the emotion in the village was so strong that the vicar decided to hold a funeral service for them. Their names were entered in Whitton's burial Register, but the funeral rites on Friday, 27 July 1906 were held, not in the Church, but in a boat moored in the River Humber above the wreck "where they are, in a manner, buried" wrote Rev. Benjamin Hunter in the Register.'

The Humber and the Ouse were notorious for having shallows in their course as they meandered. Bargemen had a dilemma. The deeper and safer channel often followed the twists of the river – but to follow such a course was time consuming. They wanted to get upriver with their cargo as quickly as possible, but didn't want to ground on a sandbank. Whilst today mariners can use echo sounders to get an accurate reading of the water's

Model of the *Selby Michael*, as made by Laurie Dews, showing the sounding rod.

(Author)

depth, on the dumb barges, there were no such luxuries. They had to use the 'sounding rod'. Laurie explains its use:

'We had a sounding rod – it was a long pole painted black and white. It was about ten foot long, with a black line at about eight foot. We'd push the rod over the side of the bow of the barge, and if we didn't feel anything by the time the black marker went under, we'd know there was at least eight foot of water, so we'd shout "Deep!"

'If it just hit we'd shout "eight foot". If we kept going and the rod grounded before the black marker got wet, we'd yell "seven foot and shordnin'". Then we'd take it careful like over the shallows and when more of the rod started to submerge we'd be able to cry out "eight foot and deepnin'". Then you'd know your barge had crossed the worst of the shallows and you could go ahead with confidence. Possibly as much as thirty minutes saved.'

Wise bargemen also knew to look out for tell tales on the river-bank. By experience, they'd know that a certain mark on a wall or branch on a tree indicated a certain depth of water in the channel. By comparing the bankside tell-tales with the reading from the sounding rod, they could get an idea of the gradation in the depth, and pass that information onto others.

'We'd look out and see maybe nine foot on Barton depth gauge, but we'd only read seven foot on the sounding rod. So we'd know it was two foot worse than Barton Board over the shallows before the tide came up and we could tell pilots and other barges about that.'

When motorized barges came into service, the canny skipper had another trick. Surfing.

'If you knew you were coming up to a shallows, there was a way over it. You'd run up to the shallows at full speed and then when you

got to the start of the shallows, you'd cut your engine to half. Because the stern was lower than the rest of the barge, you'd be building up a wash so when you cut engine speed, the wave you'd built up would sweep forward and carry you over the sandbar. If you'd tried to go at it all full speed, you'd have grounded.'

If the trick failed, and you were caught on a sandbank, problems of time and safety arose. Firstly, if the tide was ebbing and there was no longer sufficient depth for the barge to float, there was a wait of several hours for the next flood tide to increase the river's depth. That would put your payday off by perhaps another day. More worrying was the possibility of the barge breaking her back. As the barge settled on the mud and sand, the riverbed may have been uneven. Perhaps the fore and aft parts were still in water and had their weight taken by the water whilst the middle of the barge resting on the river bed had no such support. This differential support given to the cargo meant that the effect of its weight could then crack open the hull, losing both the cargo and the barge itself.

'As this area is very low lying and close to a lot of water, it can be very murky. We didn't have radar in those days, just the skipper with his compass, the mate on the forecastle as lookout and a foghorn or buzzer. One foggy night, we'd just passed Walker Dykes and were looking for Apex Light, where the Ouse and Trent meet. This light is situated in the middle of the river. I gave a blast on the buzzer when suddenly an empty Harker's tanker barge loomed up ahead, coming straight for us. Now we couldn't stop. The barges had no power, the tide was taking us upstream at seven knots, and we were going faster than that because you have to have speed over the water to be able to navigate. To change course would put us across the course of the tanker, which would be a bad idea! So, all we could do was to keep going and hope for the best. We hit him, putting a big dent in

Collision damage to the port bow of *Selby Linda.* (Laurie Dews)

his bows and he did the same for us. Both ships carried on and disappeared from each other's view into the fog. There was nothing else to do – you couldn't turn round! Luckily we both managed to get to port to show off our wounds. Ah well, never a dull moment!

'Now, past Whitton Ness railway station.'

Map of the river journey from Barton to Goole. (Alice Prince)

This was a lonely terminus of a branch of the North Lindsey Light Railway, from Scunthorpe. It opened in 1910, to connect with a packet boat sailing between Gainsborough and Hull operating three days per week. It was never very well patronised, and passenger traffic ended in 1925 with total closure in 1951.

'Next up is Apex Light at Trent Falls where the rivers Trent and Ouse diverge. Keep the Apex Light on your port side if you are travelling up the Ouse. The river currents and swell become much reduced after Apex.'

Thousands of tons of stone were tipped here in the 1930s to form so-called Training Walls to reduce the effect of the aegir or river wave. It is alleged that a gamekeeper shot by a

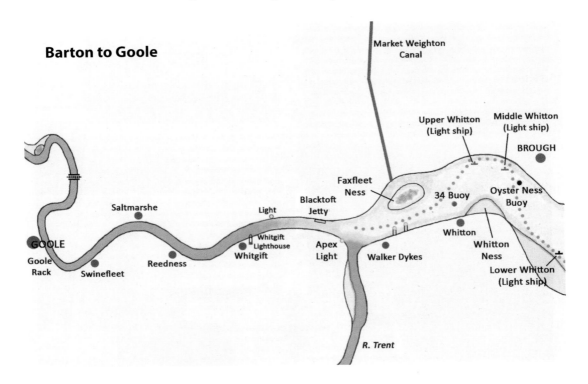

Barton to Goole

bargeman was also dumped here. The body was never found, but the man who shot him did go to prison. The light has since been removed to safe storage at the Yorkshire Waterways Museum in Goole. Passing Apex means that a vessel has now entered the Ouse

'We head up the River Ouse across the river to Blacktoft, passing Blacktoft jetty on our starboard side.

'We used to say, "Where there's a jetty, there's a pub", and at Blacktoft the Hope and Anchor was a handy place to wait in whilst the tide turned. We spent many happy hours there. The jetty had a foghorn which everyone knew as the 'Blacktoft Bull'. You could hear it for miles around when they sounded it in the mist and fog.'

BELOW:
Stone training walls surround the Apex light at the confluence of the rivers Trent and Ouse.

(Laurie Dews)

RIGHT:
Apex Light at the Yorkshire Waterways Museum, 2016.

(Author)

Blacktoft Jetty was a safe refuge for craft in foggy conditions or when water was shallow. Originally built as a timber structure in 1884, it was replaced by the more modern facility in 1967 as shown here.
(Yorkshire Waterways Museum)

The Hope and Anchor, Blacktoft, 2010. (Author)

Another tale tells of how a more famous visitor came to the jetty in 1963. The story goes that infamous Russian spy Kim Philby was whisked away from this isolated spot by a Russian cargo ship, directly to Moscow. Unfortunately, the truth is rather more mundane; Comrade P was indeed removed to the USSR by ship, but the ship departed from Beirut.

'Whitgift village is next, on the port or Lincolnshire side. Here the clock on the church has a famous "High Noon"; instead of having "XII" it has "X111" at the top of its clock face.

'Now we navigate Pile Rack, and across to the Squire of Saltmarshe's estate, passing Reedness on our port side.'

Around Swinefleet and Orchard Light a tragic accident occurred on 18 January 1961 when BOCM's tug *OCO* left Hull in the early hours towing three barges loaded with seed for the mill, but was run down by the coaster *Henfield*, rolled over and sank.

'When OCO *started rolling over, mate Fred Nelson was thrown overboard – and he couldn't swim. On a dark wintry night, and wearing a topcoat, there was little chance of survival. Mate Stodge on one of the towed barges threw a rope out. The rope had an "eye" or hoop in it - and as luck would have it, the eye landed over Fred's head and he was able to grab hold of the rope and be pulled in.*

'Fireman Spike Wadsworth was in the stokehole hatchway and was straight into the river. He managed to swim against a strong tide and make it to the shore. Trouble was the shore was lined with greasy stones and the tide kept trying to pull him off. Spike was shouting "Help!" at the top of his voice, more in desperation than hope, but it turned out he'd come ashore at the foot of someone's garden. The chap in the house and his wife were having an early breakfast at six o'clock when they heard Spike's cries, wandered down to the bottom of the garden, dragged him in, dried him down and gave him a warm breakfast. Spike made a point of going back every year to thank the couple who had saved his life.'

Extract from *Selby Times*, January 1961, describing the sinking of the tug *OCO*.
(Author)

Sadly, the other two members of the crew, skipper Jack Sumpter and Engineer Harry Jackson, weren't so lucky, and their bodies were found together at Blacktoft Jetty some time later.

'After Swinefleet we sweep round a right hand bend to come into Goole Rack. Goole Church and Water Tower come into view. We pass Ocean Lock on our port side, also Victoria Pier and Victoria Lock, then we pass Shuffleton with all the small cob boats and house boats moored along the river bank. We sometimes called this area Sleepy Hollow.'

This was where Sam had been thrown ashore as a babe all

TWO BARLBY MEN IN RIVER DRAMA
Engineer missing after B.O.C.M. tug sinks

THE Barlby engineer of the tug O.C.O., and the captain, were missing when the vessel overturned and sank after a collision in the River Ouse three miles downstream from Goole on Wednesday. The fireman, also from Barlby, and the mate were saved.

Robie pulling 4 BOCM in formation past Goole, mid 1950s. (Yorkshire Waterways Museum)

Map of the river journey from Goole to Selby. (Alice Prince)

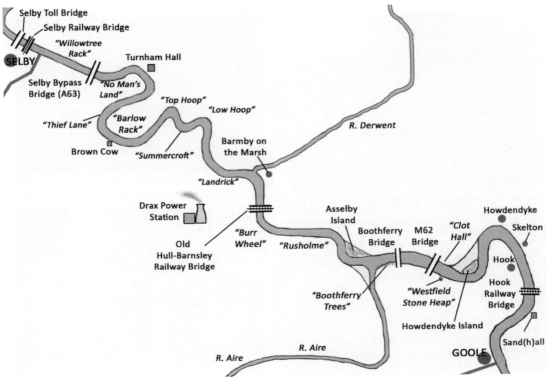

those years ago. An aerial image from the 1950s, showing *Robie* hauling four BOCM barges past Goole docks illustrates how a well-regulated convoy would appear at this stage of the journey.

'Next was Sandall. Here, before the Second World War, sand sloops would grab sand from the river bed, and when full, sail back down to Hull. When the tugs were running, they sometimes took a tow with them. It was said that Charlie Richardson and his brother would sail out of Hull on a Monday morning, and return to Hull on the Saturday. The rumour was that once they'd had a wash on Monday morning, they didn't wash again until safely back in Hull at the end of the week.

At Sandall, Robie *starts blowing on the buzzer, one long blast and six short, to ask for Goole Railway Bridge to be swung open. We called it Hook Bridge.'*

It was always tricky coming up to Hook Bridge. It followed a bend in a river and you could also be confused between the red lights of the cars on the road, or the red light of the signal on the bridge telling you if the bridge was going to open for you or not. These days you'd just radio ahead and if the bridgeman

Steam locomotive crossing Hook Bridge, as seen from a barge.
(Yorkshire Waterways Museum)

informs you that you have to wait for a train to cross, you'd just cut back on the throttle. Back in the dumb barge days life wasn't so simple.

'When you're coming up round the bend to Hook Bridge at seven knots on a spring tide with four barges on and each carrying over 200 tons you blow for the bridge and hope it'll swing for you. But if the bridgeman puts up a red flag you can't just stop. You've got to turn the barges around and hold them against the tide. Then watch out for a green flag to tell you the bridge is being swung and turn 'em again. Then you've got to get speed up because the barges have to be going faster than the tide to get their tillers to work. You've got to be able to steer the barge or you could get smashed against the breakwaters on the bridge pillars. You have to watch out when the tug turns your barge around 'cos the tiller will swing like mad and it's got enough behind it to knock a man clean over the side of the barge.'

Steering through Hook Railway Bridge was tricky and dangerous especially if it was a Spring tide, because the tide would set vessels down onto the east abutment. Many times have barges been swept down onto that abutment. This is not the last time on the journey that bargemen have to be aware of the way that a current caused by a bridge support causes problems to keeping a barge on course. The effect is dealt with in detail in the section concerning the passage of the bridges in Selby.

'After passing safely through the bridge, the village of Skelton is on the starboard side and Howden Dyke with its fertilizers factory and Scarr's Shipyard which had a slipway for pulling barges up for repair.'

Scarr's shipyard was begun in 1902 and was at its busiest just after the First World War. The firm built some of BOCMs dumb barges before closure came, after many takeovers, in 1994.

'On our port side are Hook petrol jetty where Goole's petrol barges discharged into the large Cleveland storage tanks. Cooks and Harkers of Knottingley used to trade here too. Next is Howden Dyke Island in the middle of the river.'

The effects of shallows and summer and winter currents were well known here.

The City of York Engineer, Mr A. Creer produced this map for a report to the Navigation Committee in 1906. Along with

Chart of river flow around Howdendyke, 1906. (Author)

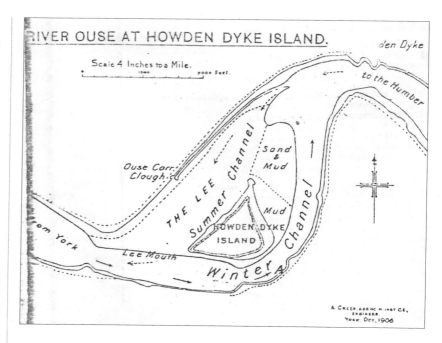

the map, Mr Creer described the problems with navigation channels most eloquently:

'When the river is in its good state, as it should be in March and April a very large volume of tidal water enters the river between Selby and Naburn. This volume, along with river water, is sufficient to sweep back into the lower reaches (of the Ouse) and into the Humber a large volume of warp (silt) brought up by the flood (tide). However, gradually the volume of water assisting the ebb in its beneficent work is reduced owing to the absence of rain.

'When this stage is reached the evil results soon become apparent. The warp brought up by each flood deposits its quota on the river bed. Although not perceptible at first this gradual accretion raises the bed, reducing the space available for flood waters and rendering the river less able to clear itself. This deterioration continues until a heavy flood (tide) enables the upland portion of the river to regain its ascendency and sweep back the deposited accumulations. In the Ouse not only do we have a river with a distinct summer and winter condition, but also with summer and winter channels.'

'If the water had flowed high enough, we would pass the Island on our port side, meaning a shorter trip, but seeing there wasn't enough

*water "over the middle", we had to go round the island leaving it on
our starboard side, passing the Hospital Bight, so-called as there was
a hospital just over the bank.'*

Whilst the situation may seem clear on a map, in the featureless
flat landscape around the Humber, it could be very difficult to
decide which channel to follow.

*'This area was also popular with duck shooters and sometimes seals
could be seen basking on the sands. Next came Westfield stone heap
which had a red light on it, and Westfield Hospital and across a stretch
of the river we call Clot Hall. This was a very shallow part of the river.
In summertime there could be as little as two to three feet of water in
the river here at low tide.'*

This is where the M62 now crosses the Ouse. Begun in 1973 it
opened in 1976 to complete the main 109-mile length of the M62.
To starboard were many wrecks of old wooden keels and sloops

Selby Michael towing
Selby Cygnus towards
Hull, near Clot Hall,
1976. The craft have
just gone under the
M62 bridge, and
Boothferry Bridge is
in the background.
(Laurie Dews)

A more modern view of the M62 bridge and navigation light.
(Author)

which have come to grief and have been pulled up on the bank to rot, and in so doing reinforce the bank against erosion.

'*One of the barges belonged to my grandfather, Bill. This was the final resting place of the* Sam. *She had been crushed at Goole jetty in the incident that nearly killed the family. Bill had just bought her and he hadn't got her fully insured and so he lost everything.*

'*Next, blow for Boothferry Bridge, one long blast and six short blasts again. There's no bother with this bridge, they swing it almost straightaway. After passing safely under the bridge we pass the ferry houses on the starboard side.*

'*The ferry was something like a pontoon pulled across with ropes or chains.*'

The ferry, like all of them in this part of the river, belonged to the Archbishop of Durham. It was replaced by the bridge in 1929.

'*We now pass Boothferry Trees on our port side and when Everard's oil tankers came down the river from Selby loaded with oil, and the water had ebbed away too low, they used to stop against the river bank at Boothferry Trees because it was a deep water riding berth. This meant the ship would stay afloat throughout the ebb tide. Originally ships had to moor to one of the trees with a rope, so the man whose land the trees were on said that Mr Everard who owned the ships had to buy one.*

'*Next on our journey we pass the mouth of the River Aire which goes to Leeds and on our starboard side is Asselby Island which used to be an island until the 1940s but is now joined to the mainland.*'

Asselby Island also once had channels whose course varied with the seasons, as at Howdendyke and Read's Island. Mr Greer was equally scathing about the warp here. By Laurie's time the narrower one had completely silted up.

'We come round a sweeping left hand bend and we are now into Rusholme Rack which ends when we come to a sharp right hand bend called Burr Wheel.'

Tug and barges passing through Boothferry Bridge.
(Susan Butler/ Howdenshire History)

The ferry at Booth.
(Susan Butler/ Howdenshire History)

Rusholme was recorded as a farmhouse in 1822. It now enjoys views of a wind farm and cooling towers.

'Directly in front of us now is Barmby Railway Bridge, another one long blast and six short on the tug's buzzer and the bridge again swings for us to pass through.'

Barmby Bridge was also known as the Long Drax swing bridge. It was built in the 1880s for the Hull and Barnsley Railway. The H&BR was formed relatively late for a railway company, and its raison d'être was effectively to speed coal to the coast and supply raw materials to south Yorkshire. As such it struck a fairly direct line between Hull and Barnsley, but because other railway companies had already taken the most advantageous routes, the H&BR were forced into building a bridge across the Ouse around twice as lengthy as the North Eastern Railway's one (built 1840, replaced 1891) at Selby. Both bridges were elegant swing bridges with a metal bowstring lattice structure and a high central cabin giving clear views of river and rail traffic. At Barmby, the span was 400ft, giving two opening spans of around 100ft. The H&BR was not economically successful, and the line closed in 1968, but the bridge was not dismantled at once. For over sixty years, there had been many plans for a road bypass for Selby, and one idea was to use this rail bridge, suitably altered as a road bridge for a Selby bypass. This plan came to naught, and the graceful structure was dismantled in late 1976.

By the time Barmby was reached, the river was much narrower than it was at Goole, but a 100ft opening span remained

The former Hull & Barnsley Railway Bridge at Barmby.
(Susan Butler/ Howdenshire History)

sufficient to allow the squadron of four barges to pass.

'We pass Barmby village on our starboard side and Long Drax on our port side. The voyage continues until we come to another sharp bend, Low Hoop, and into Summercroft Reach. On our port side is a farm that used to belong to a Quaker family and the family graves and some grave stones are in the garden. Others have been moved to rest behind the old Quaker Meeting House off Gowthorpe in Selby.'

Quaker memorial from Summercroft, now in Selby. (Author)

Drax Priory was founded by William Paynel in the 1130s, during the reign of Selby-born Henry I. Four hundred years and seven Henrys later, the Priory was closed during the Dissolution of the Monasteries. The Priory buildings became a farm and a meeting place for the Society of Friends (Quakers). The remaining religious buildings were demolished in 1953. In the early 1970s, some gravestones were relocated to a site behind Selby's main street, Gowthorpe, and the area has been dedicated to the people of the town by the Society of Friends.

The site in Drax remains a Scheduled Ancient Monument. Summercroft is a nearby isolated farm house.

'The next sharp turn is known as Top Hoop and now we are into Barlow Rack, and at the other end of Barlow Rack is Brown Cow which

Buildings on Drax Abbey site, 1930s.

got its name from a little pub that used to be there, but it is now a private house and brewery. People say that wherever there was a staithe or landing, there'll be a pub, so maybe there was a jetty to go with the pub here.'

Barlow had a brief connection with a more exotic form of transport, the airship. For around a dozen years between 1915 and 1930, Barlow had an outstation of the airship construction works at nearby Howden. The airship R33 was built there by Armstrong Whitworth, the famous Newcastle-based heavy engineering company in 1919.

'Thief Lane is close by, so maybe there was a smuggling connection too. The next bend we come to is Thief Lane End and into another part of the river which is known as No Man's Friend. It got its name from the old keel and sloop men who used to sail up and down the river because if you were sailing up the river with a fair wind, when you got to No Man's Friend, the river bent right round so that you had a head wind, which was, of course, not a very friendly blast!

'When we got round that bend we came to Turnham Hall on our starboard and Roscarrs Farm on our port side.'

There has been a manor house of one sort or another at Turnham since the fourteenth century. In the fifteenth, the locality was so rascally that John Pylkington was given a licence to crenelate (fortify) the Hall. The current building dates originally from the early nineteenth century.

'The next twist in the river's course leads us into Willow Tree Rack, with Cherry Orchard Farm on the starboard along with the jetties for Sturge Chemicals in the distance. This is the outskirts of Selby, and time for work on the tow ropes.'

J&E Sturge were major chemical manufacturers. Their Selby plant was a leading supplier of citric acid, an important chemical feedstock and food additive. They were another firm who used the river to obtain their raw materials, mainly shiploads of molasses which were the raw material from which the citric acid was produced. From Laurie's point of view, the presence of Sturge's jetties, possibly with vessels tied up meant a further restriction in the width of the river.

Chapter 10

COMING INTO SELBY AND THE PASSAGE OF THE BRIDGES

W illow Tree Rack is the last stretch of the river before Selby that is straight enough to allow the complicated practice of 'singling out' to be achieved. For the journey from Hull thus far, the tug has pulled the barges along in pairs, as seen in the aerial picture at Goole. With lengths of rope around 100 feet long, and the barges themselves being of similar length, the whole assembly is around 400 feet or an eighth of a mile long. The barges were about twenty feet wide, and allowing for clear water to let the wash from the tug escape, the convoy was about sixty feet wide.

Whilst these dimensions were not a problem in the lower parts of the river, by the time that the outskirts of Selby had been reached, the river had narrowed from being almost a mile wide at Hull to less than a tenth of that at Willow Tree Rack. As the

Willow Tree Rack 2011. (Author)

river narrowed, so did the width of the openings available at various swing bridges to allow the barges to pass. Hook, Boothferry and Barmby bridges needed careful navigation to avoid the barges being dragged towards the bridge supports, but had sufficient width to allow the convoy to pass. This was not the case for the passage at Selby. Here, the Railway Swing bridge opened to allow a channel around eighty feet wide, whilst the Old Toll Bridge's passage was less than half that.

On the approach to Selby, works jetties and wharves on the port side in 1937, and later at Sturge's, Tate and Lyle on the starboard, along with Cochrane's and Connell's shipyards made the navigable channel still narrower.

Willow Tree Rack was the place to put the barges in single file. This was singling out, which required smart work from the bargemen. The barges had no power of their own, just the momentum provided by the pull of the tug. Be that as it may, the barges were still moving upstream at least at the pace of the tide. At the correct moment, the tug's mate would strike the tow rope from his port hook. The two barges that were joined to the port side tow were now merely drifting forward whilst the other pair were still being pulled.

The mate on the leading port-side barge must now rapidly haul 120 feet of soaking and possibly icy rope in, whilst standing on a deck that's possibly awash with icy water. No sooner has he done this then he has to heave that rope to the rear starboard barge as it was being pulled by. That rope is then secured to the aft of the barge and the two loose barges were pulled into line, and all four barges are in line. Now it was time to navigate Selby's two bridges.

'When all the ropes are taut, "All tight" is shouted out and the tug skipper blows one long, long, long blast and six short on the buzzer. This is the request for bridge opening.

'Before we get to the bridges we pass the Sugar Factory on the starboard or Barlby side and Cochrane's

Close up view of tow rope on hook.
(Laurie Dews)

1. *Two pairs of barges are pulled in parallel formation.*

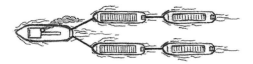

2. *The port-side rope to the bottom pair is released setting them adrift.*

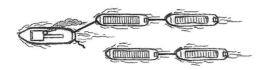

3. *A new rope is thrown to the drifting barges.*

4. *The barges are now in single file.*

Diagram of the singling out process.

(Alice Prince)

shipyard on the port side, with their vessels ready to be launched into the Ouse. The river isn't wide enough for a traditional bow- or stern-first launch, so ships slid down the stocks sideways. As you can imagine, that created a heck of a wave. Folk used to watch the launch from the opposite or Barlby Bank - and sometimes they got a bit of a soaking. In later years, as the boats being built got larger, Cochrane's would warn people not to watch amidships. On one occasion in the early 1970s I was watching, and a woman who was watching from amidships was caught by a wave that came over the bank, was swept her off her feet under a parked car. I had to run and drag her out from underneath the car before she drowned.'

The 2,200 ton *Superiority* being launched at Cochrane's in 1990. A vessel of this size could easily produce a 'launch wave' that would overtop the far bank.

(Ye Olde Fraternitie of Selebians)

In the 1930s Cochrane's built trawlers, before contributing many vessels to the war effort, then a variety of bulk carriers, fishing vessels for the Humber fleets and ferries for UK service, until their closure in 1992.

'Once the superstructure of these trawlers was complete, they would be towed down to Hull to have engines fitted. One particular vessel caused a lot of problems whilst being towed on this voyage, and she kept running into the river bank. On returning from Hull, the tug skipper met Mr Cochrane who told him, "You seem to have had a bit of trouble with our ship as you ran her into the river bank." The skipper considered the situation and replied, "Well Mr Cochrane, that's what the river banks are for – to stop ships getting out of the river!"

'On the Selby side, flanking the entrance to the Selby Canal is Rostron's paper mill and then another of Selby's shipyards, Connell's Shipyard and Dry Dock. The last barge to be built there was called the Selebian in the early 1930s, and it eventually worked for Whitaker's of Hull, last seen hauling paper onto Selby Canal for Rostron's.'

The *Bradman* making a big splash on launch in October 1936.

(Ye Olde Fraternitie of Selebians)

Rostron's was a company that produced paper and cardboard products. Latterly named Rigid Paper, the site closed in 2009. The remnants of the firm's name picked out in white enamel in the boundary wall still remain. Connell's yard also maintained the breakwaters on the bridges and remained in business until the 1950s. It is said that Mr Connell had an idiosyncratic way of settling pay disputes. Should a worker wish for an increase in his pay rate, the procedure was simple. If Mr C. disagreed, it was a matter of stepping out into the yard and literally fighting for ones pay. 'To the victor the spoils' indeed. Having passed these works, there are now jetties to port.

'Now we pass the York Corporation jetties. One customer here was sometimes the Sir Malcolm Campbell. *This was a War Department ship, that carried ordnance for the stores at York.'*

The bargemen would now have to deal with the first of Selby's two swing bridges. To the port side is the railway jetty, with its hustle and bustle making the navigable channel more confused.

Ahead is the nineteenth-century bridge that allows the Hull and Selby railway to cross the Ouse. The original rail bridge of 1840 was a bascule bridge which opened in a vertical plane like

A busy river scene just below Selby Rail Bridge. (Richard Moody)

Tower Bridge in London, but by 1891 it had become too weak for the increased weight of trains passing on what was then the London to Edinburgh East Coast Main Line. The replacement bridge swung – and still swings – in the horizontal plane. The Act of Parliament that authorized its construction stipulated that it had to be able to open fully within a minute. This feat was originally achieved by the action of hydraulic motors, but now acts electrically.

Of more importance to bargemen was the fact that the Act authorizing the new bridge reversed the rights of way at the bridge. In 1840, river traffic was so regular and rail services so sparse that boats had priority. Fifty years later, however, the situation was reversed, and boats had to request that the bridge opened – and if a train was coming, that request would be refused. In such a situation, the rounding up procedure described earlier at Hook came into play – only on this occasion made more difficult as the chain of barges was now twice as lengthy. At the time, as there was no radio communication between barge and bridge, a barge skipper didn't know if the bridge would open. Instead, the bridge had coloured signals which bargemen called spectacles, which were similar to the coloured filters used in semaphore signals on the railway.

'The railway jetty with its coal chute was where the tugs could get their bunkers filled. The goods station was just across Ousegate from

the jetties. A man with a red flag marched into the middle of the carriageway to halt traffic as a full coal wagon was hauled across Ousegate onto the railway jetty. To deliver the coal the wagon bottom was "knocked out" and the coal shot down the chute into the tug's bunker hold.

'When the signal on the railway bridge which looks like a pair of spectacles drops we know that they are swinging the Railway Bridge open for us. Once past the railway bridge, you'd give one long blast then you steamed through the Toll Bridge.'

Motorized barge passing through Selby Railway bridge.
(Richard Moody)

Selby's second bridge, some 200 yards upstream and built a century earlier, is for the A19/A63 road crossing. The Toll Bridge, as it is universally known, although tolls were removed in 1991, was begun in 1791, and also swings open in the horizontal plane. River traffic always had right of way over road vehicles, so as soon as the rail bridge began to swing, the road men began to open theirs as well.

As described earlier, the road bridge had a much narrower opening than the rail bridge. With a fully-loaded twenty-foot-wide barge travelling at least six knots, trying to get through a

Vista of the Ouse at Selby. This vista shows a vessel approaching the already-opened railway swing bridge, with the road bridge in the foreground just beginning to open. On the right-hand bank between the bridges, Williamson's jetty is still functional, with the railway jetty across Ousegate from the entrance to the old station, just this side of the rail bridge. Beyond lies the entrance to the Selby Canal and the horizontal steelwork of Cochrane's Shipyard. Sturge's jetty is obscured by the roof line of houses on the left bank. Beyond the industry, Willow Tree Rack stretches out.

Tug *Robie* and barge *Selby Pollux* between Selby's bridges, with OCO offices to the left, beyond Williamson's wharf, on Ousegate.
(www.oldbarnsley.com)

gap that's less than forty feet wide – in other words just ten feet between barge and bridge – a steady and firm hand really was needed on the tiller! The Act authorizing the bridge also required that the vessels shall not be interrupted in their passage and that they shall have right of way over foot traffic. This was usually taken to require the channel to be clear in 30 seconds or so. Certainly with only 200 yards or so between the railway and road bridges, a rapid swing was vital.

Until a new bridge was put in place in 1970, the swing was done purely by muscle power, turning a large cogged wheel. Electric motors were installed to work the new bridge but the original wheels are still to be seen on the wall of the bridge-men's house.

Perſon oʒ Perſons appointed by and at the Expence of the ſaid Company of Propʒietoʒs, oʒ their Succeſ-ſoʒs, in ſuch Manner that Ueſſels may not at any Time be interrupted in paſſing the ſaid Bʒidge; and that Ueſſels ſhall at all Times have a Pʒeference of paſſing thʒough the ſame, to Paſſengers going over the ſaid Bʒidge; and ſuch Ueſſels ſhall take their Turns in the Courſe as they arrive, having Occaſion to paſs thʒough

LX. And be it further enacted, That a clear Opening ſhall be left in the ſaid Bʒidge, foʒ the Paſſage of Ueſ-ſels, of not leſs than Thirty-one Feet, to be properly ſituated oʒ placed towards the Barlby Side of the ſaid River, where there ſhall be a ſufficient Depth of Water foʒ the Purpoſes of the ſaid Navigation, accoʒding to the true Meaning of this Act; and the ſaid Company of Pʒopʒietoʒs, and their Succeſſoʒs, ſhall cauſe the Leaf oʒ Leaves of the ſaid Bʒidge to be made and executed,

The aftermath of the collision of the *Agility* with Selby Toll Bridge, May 1930. Note the queue for the ferry to the left of the picture. The 1791 Act stipulated that the Toll Bridge Company had to provide a ferry should the bridge be unusable. (Laurie Dews)

Cog wheels formerly used to operate Selby Toll Bridge, now mounted on side of Bridgeman's cottage. (Author)

Barges passing Selby
Toll Bridge, 1968.
(Richard Moody)

'When we were lads we used to hang around the Toll Bridge and wait to see if any barges were coming through. If they were and the bridge needed swinging, sometimes the men would let us work the wheels to open the span. It was hard work, mind, but we did get paid half a crown for our trouble.'

Navigation wasn't as simple as pointing the bow of the barge at the gap. By this stage the river had narrowed to less than 200 feet wide, and there was the constant danger of falling athwart. On a few occasions, the bridge came off worse than the barge. This was famously the case in May 1930, when the inappropriately-named *Agility* didn't live up to her name and smashed the bridge decking off the supports. In keeping with the requirements of the Act, the bridge company had to reinstate a ferry whilst the decking was repaired. Continual, although not quite as catastrophic, collisions such as this were the cause for the replacement of the original bridge in 1969–70.

Harry Speight (R) and Laurie Dews (in cabin) on board the 'Selby Tony' as it passes under Selby Toll Bridge on the way upriver to the Barlby jetties. Note the girth of the rope in the foreground that the mate has to deal with. Beyond the bridge, note Williamson's wharf: the site of the housing development of 2015. (Laurie Dews)

Even if the worst came to the worst and the craft did sink, salvage was still an option, but not always a successful one.

'At Williamson's Wharf on our port side, sloops used to bring bricks from Gilberdyke and Newport Brickworks up the Weighton River. One didn't quite make its delivery. It was dragged aside by the river currents and lay athwart the bridge, then smashed against the breakwaters and sank. Skipper and crew clambered clear, and there were still hopes for the cargo. A simple job – just wait for the ebb tide, run a cable underneath the hull and lift the barge.

'The only problem was that it was a wooden barge and the cable was steel. As soon as the cable started to take the weight it was too much for the wooden hull which broke in two. As far as I know 200 tons of best East Riding bricks are on the river bed – but the river broke up the barge over the next few tides.'

MOORING UP AND UNLOADING AT BARLBY

Once beyond the Toll Bridge, the concerns about navigation weren't at an end. No more than 400 yards upstream, Scots Bight is a 120° bend to starboard, giving little sight of any oncoming vessels. However, just around the bend was where the OCO/BOCM wharves lay, so journey's end was close, but further boat-handling skills were required.

'Above the Toll Bridge on the port bow is Spillers' Swan flour mill, also the Ideal flour mill and just in the bight is Scott's oil mill, where the sloop Sprite, *captained by John Gledhall, discharged cottonseed until 1939. This was the last sail-powered trading ship on this part of the Ouse.*

Also on the port side was a much older trading point – the medieval Abbots' Staithe. This was the mighty stone-built warehouse where goods and materials that the Abbey traded

Dumb barges towed upriver of Selby Toll Bridge, approaching Scott's bight. *Leeds Jupiter* is nearest the camera. The barges have been singled out.

(www.oldbarnsley.com)

Motorized barges upriver of Selby Toll Bridge circa 1968, approximately forty years later than the previous picture.
(Laurie Dews)

were stored. This facility had been in place since at least the fourteenth century. This part of the river is also where the ferry plied its course in the days before the Toll Bridge.

'Having passed through the Toll Bridge, we now have to berth. This could be a tricky manoeuvre depending on the state of the tide and the availability of mooring points.'

In the early part of Laurie's career, there were no jetties and mooring up required considerable skill in a procedure known as 'mooring head and tails'. Even when proper jetties were constructed, this technique could come into play if the factory was busy. Wherever the barges were moored, industrial technology in the shape of an overhead railway, a runway and bucket elevators, latterly with vacuum pumps all came into play to empty the cargo as rapidly as possible. After all, time was money and the sooner the hold was emptied, the sooner the skipper could get paid.

'It was only possible to moor up at Barlby for two hours either side of high tide. Before the jetty was built around 1937 or if there was no berth available there, vessels had to moor "heads and tails" against the river bank. Once we got past Scott's mill, we all let go of the tow ropes and hauled them in on the deck side. Being unpowered, the barges now ran upstream with the current. The mate went to the fo'c'sle deck to lower the anchor which turned the barge around, and ran it into the

river bank, putting the barge head to the incoming tide. Once it had grounded, a line was thrown and secured ashore and the anchor dropped at the stern. The other barges drifted upstream with the tide until the tide turned.

'Once that happened they returned downstream. As they passed the secured vessel, a rope was thrown to the barge that was already moored. The "moored mate" pulled on this rope, dragging the fore end of the drifting barge into the river bank, and again, an anchor dropped at the stern. Once they had formed a pair, more ropes were fixed to fix the barges together. With two anchors holding the barges off the bank, resisting movement, whichever direction the tide was running and two ropes tied to chain rings or even sturdy trees ashore, the barges were now secure. When all ropes were fast, the two mates off the two barges would go to Olympia Mills workshop to get a "footing plank". This was a long piece of timber used as a gangplank, which also helped to keep the barges off the bank. There were chains fastened into the bank, with rings for the barges to moor on to along the low side of Kirby's Mill.

'Once the jetties had been constructed, the process was simpler. With the tide still running up towards York, a man ashore would shout from the river bank to tell us all where to moor.

'Some barges would be directed to a berth to discharge. The tow rope was detached from the tug. Under just its own momentum, the flow of the river and the influence of the tiller on the barge, the skipper steered his vessel into the jetty, had ropes thrown ashore which were then secured to bollards

'Even when the jetties had been built, they could only deal with 3 vessels at a time. If you weren't wanted at once, you had to moor up heads and tails until required, against the Olympia Hotel. However you were moored, unloading could begin.'

Unloading could be by bucket elevator, electric runway, or later by vacuum pump. The elevator had many buckets on a continuous loop. It would be lowered into the barge's hold and would start to scoop all the seed out. The seed scoops mentioned in the inventory of the *Taurus* were vital here. Representatives from both the mill and the barge had to be present, which could cause a bit of friction. The owner of the barge worked four hours and then had to stand by all day and night to open more hold space or cover the barge up if it rained.

The mill men worked eight hours but the bargemen who lived on board were there in attendance all the time.

'If two elevators were lowered into the hold of a barge containing 225 tons of nuts it would take about two hours to empty, needing four men from the mill trimming the seed into the bucket and with the help of two bargemen. For one elevator, two men from the mill would join the crew and unloading would take around three hours.'

Once the buckets were full, they went round a loop before being tipped out onto an endless belt which carried the material across Barlby Road and into a silo.

This could be a terribly dusty business, especially with a cargo like cotton seed. Workers at Scott's mill had a problem with the dust raised from manually shifting the seed. Many workers developed respiratory diseases in the days before the Second World War, when simple safety measures such as dust masks were not mandatory. The vacuum pumps were an adaption of this system. Instead of having to manually shovel and level the seed in the bucket, the vacuum pipes were giant suction tubes like vacuum cleaners which sucked the cargo direct from the hold on to the belt.

'If the barge was loaded with a bagged commodity it would have to moor under the runway berth, which was an overhead electric runway. This was a marvellous device which ran on overhead rails which came all the way from inside the factory.'

A man sat inside a cabin suspended from the rails overhead, beneath which was an empty board with hooks at each corner. When he got over the hold of the barge, the board was lowered and then one mill

Laurie Dews (left) and mate Harry Sleight having partly unloaded the hold of copra. Note the seed shovels on the cargo.
(Laurie Dews)

Selby Michael joins two other Selby barges under the vacuum elevators, 1962/63. (Laurie Dews)

man and one bargeman in the hold loaded a ton of meal on the board. That would probably be twenty sacks, each weighing a hundredweight (56lb, 25kg).

'When the board was full, the chains were secured to the board and the runway driver heaved the board up and into the mill, where it was unloaded in a reverse of the way it was loaded.'

This was repeated until the barge was empty, taking about eight hours – or one mill man's shift – to unload 150 tons. That might not sound much, but 150 board-loads in eight hours is at least fifteen boards an hour or one every four minutes. If there were

LEFT: Cargo in sacks being taken out of a barge's hold at Barlby.
(Laurie Dews)

RIGHT: Cargo in sacks 'on the board' on the overhead railway at Barlby in the 1940s.
(Laurie Dews)

two of you filling that board with twenty sacks, that meant each of you hefting two hundredweight sacks of meal a minute. For eight hours straight.

'*Sometimes some of the lads were a bit cruel to the bloke in the cabin. A few of them had air rifles, and as the board was swinging round, they'd take a pot shot at the cabin or the board. The operator played merry hell, but there wasn't much he could do about it.*'

Once the barge was unloaded, there was the possibility of a return cargo. This was usually 'slab' or cattle cake, the fibrous, compressed remnants of the seed once oil had been extracted, excellent feed for livestock.

'*The barge was loaded under the runway, and the cake came out of the factory on boards, a ton at a time. It was taken off the boards three cakes at a time and stowed carefully by a bargeman and a mill man. You had to be careful stowing the cake as it crumbled easily at the edges, and the buyers didn't go for crumbled cake. If we did have one where the edges looked a bit rough, we tried to hide it between two good cakes.*'

Even if there wasn't a return load for Hull, the skipper and mate had to put all the covers and hatches on before leaving BOCM and 'dropping down' to the Selby jetties to await the tug to Hull. This simple-sounding manoeuvre called for more skilful bargecraft.

The currents, bends and proximity of other craft at Selby are potentially treacherous. Thus the river navigation by laws are strict yet clear. 'Vessels must only pass Selby Toll Bridge at slack water, against the stream or going astern with the stream,' that is, letting the current take the flow, but with the engine operating against the current to allow control if necessary. It is further advised to have an anchor ready to deploy to drag against the power of the current.

'We then had to drop the barge stern-first down river through both bridges. The captain had the tiller and the mate had to heave the anchor using anchor levers. The drag of the anchor allowed controlled steering. The anchor chains had hydraulics, but nothing was easy. If there was flood water coming down river you could have 15 fathoms (90feet, 30m) of chain out – and believe me it wasn't easy pulling that lot in. Under normal circumstances, we'd moor up at the Railway Jetty, ready for the cycle to start again, with the tow back down to Hull.'

Empty barges would complete the round trip back to Hull, but a load full of cake meant an interesting meander through Hull Docks. The laden barges would anchor up off the Minerva Pier, ready for a tow by Whitaker's tugs.

'The tug Wilberfoss *or* Cawood *would tow us into Old Harbour on the River Hull. The tug would let go of the rope before we got to Salthouse Lane bridge. After that we'd use the anchor to turn the barge around to go under North Bridge, Scott Street and then Chapman Street bridges. Wilmington Rail Bridge was a bit lower, so if we couldn't get through we'd shout "Brig ahoy" – and the bridgeman would ring his bell, put a chain across the road and swing the bridge for us. Just beyond here was our destination – Butter Mill, Kato 2 or BOCM Hull as it was called. To unload the cake onto boards – three cakes at a time – we needed two mill men and two bargemen, two to a board.'*

As always, time was money, and sometimes Sam tired of these complex manoeuvres to get around the docks in Hull, especially if only small loads had to be moved between different ships. If

Barges *Selby Richard* and *Selby Peter* moored up in thick ice at the Railway Jetty.
(Waterways World)

that was the case, Sam occasionally loaded up the cob boat with the cargo and sculled across to where the cargo was needed, saving all the shouting, bridge swinging and physical effort needed to move the whole barge around the dock with boathook and warping line. After the hold was emptied, subsequent movements depended on the tide, this time in the River Hull

'Once emptied the shipping agents would send a man to help us drop down to the low end of the harbour whilst the river was still ebbing, so we could get under the bridges. Once there a tug would tow us to another part of the Docks for our next cargo, unless we had to go into Dry Dock for repair. Whitakers had two dry docks in Hull, Lime Street and Garrison.'

One final job that the bargemen had in Selby was that of an ice-breaker. The Ouse often froze over in Laurie's day, when the tug was employed to act as an ice breaker. Once the motorized craft came in, it became another job for the barge skipper.

'Of course, weather could play its part, and sometimes winters were so cold that the river froze over. When it did, it was my job, all night, going up and down the river to make a passage and the only way you could break the ice was going through it stern first. You couldn't go head first into it 'cause you climbed on top of it. And once you climbed *on top of it, that's it. So what you had to do, you used to go stern first and the propeller used to chop all the ice up and make a channel.'*

After all that effort, what was it all for? An OCO advert from 1947 summarizes things nicely.

OCO advert from the *Selby Times* of 1947.
(Author)

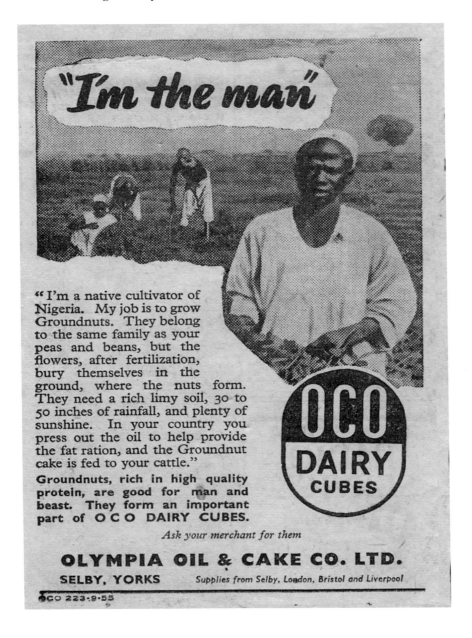

"I'm the man"

" I'm a native cultivator of Nigeria. My job is to grow Groundnuts. They belong to the same family as your peas and beans, but the flowers, after fertilization, bury themselves in the ground, where the nuts form. They need a rich limy soil, 30 to 50 inches of rainfall, and plenty of sunshine. In your country you press out the oil to help provide the fat ration, and the Groundnut cake is fed to your cattle."

Groundnuts, rich in high quality protein, are good for man and beast. They form an important part of O C O DAIRY CUBES.

Ask your merchant for them

OCO DAIRY CUBES

OLYMPIA OIL & CAKE CO. LTD.

SELBY, YORKS   *Supplies from Selby, London, Bristol and Liverpool*

OCO 223·9·55

The entire Selby river trading experience can be seen on this aerial shot of Selby, from an approximately southern direction, taken in the mid-1980s.

A: *Entrance to the Selby Canal*
B: *York Corporation Jetty*
C: *Railway stations with railway jetty on bank*
D: *Railway Swing Bridge*
E: *Williamson's Wharf*
F: *Selby Toll Bridge (as it was at the time)*
G: *Site of Abbots' Staithe*
H: *Ideal Flour Mill (now Westmill Foods)*
I: *Scott's Bight*
J: *Company housing*
K: *BOCM jetties*
L: *BOCM factory*
M: *River Ouse (going north towards York)*
N: *Railway line going east to Hull.*

From the mouth of the canal to Scott's Bight is about half a mile.

A further view of BOCM's operation can be seen in the second photograph, from the north.

A: *Trackbed of Former East Coast Main Line railway to York*
B: *Tank farm*
C: *Riverside crane*
D: *Boxed-in conveyors traversing the main road*
E: *Barges being unloaded under the elevator*
F: *Empty barges laid up on the river bank*
G: *Main body of the BOCM factory*
H: *Railway line to Hull*

Chapter 12

GETTING PAID FOR THE JOB

The 'payment by thirds' method of pay that beguiled Bill Dews to throw his lot in with Soapy Joe remained in play for much of the time that Laurie worked on the dumb barges. OCO/BOCM owned the barges and paid for all the ropes, covers, paint and tackle needed to run the show. As the inventory for the Virgo showed, the amount of kit was extensive. The company would also pay for regular maintenance, but not if the skipper was culpable for an accident. There were also the costs involved in registering the barge for use on the river, an annual fee a little like car tax.

The day-to-day costs were met by the skipper. Once payment was received for cargo carried, he paid out for any brokerage, dock or towing dues. That left a net figure, out of which the company took a third, the skipper the remaining two thirds. This didn't all go into his back pocket, but rather had to fund the mate's wages, along with any incidental costs such as slipping some money to the lock keeper at Hull or to pay for coal for the fires in the cabin. As Laurie's wartime anecdote showed, bargemen weren't above a little skulduggery to reduce that fuel expenditure. Sam's log shows that working his boat in the 1920s brought in a gross annual income of around £275. After taking account of perhaps £25 for fees and charges, and

Official description of the *Selby Michael*.

DESCRIPTION of the Motor Tug in respect of which this Licence is granted

Official Number under Merchant Shipping Act.	301644	Number of Licence		Name of Motor Tug	SELBY MICHAEL	
Port Number and Year of Registry	1960/ Hull	Port of Registry	Hull	Registered Tonnage 106.50	How Propelled Single Screw	Framework Steel
		No. of Engines	Description	When Made	Diameter of Cylinders	Length of Stroke	No. of Horses' power combined
Particulars of Engines		One	Internal combustion and 3/1 reduction gear Four stroke single acting	Gardiner Diesel 1960	5½"	7¾"	7.56 n.h.p. 95.0 b.h.p.

Annual registration document for *Selby Michael* in 1960.

(Laurie Dews)

No. 9063

Certificate of Payment of Registration Dues.
RIVER CRAFT.

Humber Conservancy Board,

Date 28st September 1960

Received of the British Oil. Cake mills Ltd .

Barlly Road. Selby   Owners of the
                                          Agents

Selby michael   of   Selby   the sum of

_____ pounds, _____ shillings and _____ pence,

the amount of Registration Dues payable to the Humber Conservancy Board for the

year ending 31st December, 1960.

Class matot Jessel   Nom. H.P.   8

                                  J. CHADWICK

                            H. COLQUHOUN,

£   - : 15 : -   Chief Collector.

the profit that the company would take, Sam was left with around £170 a year for himself, out of which he had to pay his mate. Accurate figures are difficult to come by, but according to a Hansard report of a parliamentary debate of wages in the early part of the 1920s, average annual wages for a labourer were £45 per year and an able seaman about £65. Assuming Sam paid his mate at those kind of levels Sam himself received about £120 per annum. At the time, Hansard reports that a locomotive driver averaged £125 per year, so Sam was paid at a level equivalent to other skilled manual workers of the time.

Whilst Sam and Elisabeth had a house, some of the mates saved money by living on board.

'*Many of the men who worked as mates had no homes and they knew when they got a job as a mate on one of the barges at least they had a cabin in the fo'c'sle and a bed and a fire to keep them warm. They certainly worked hard for their keep! Life on a barge was very hard in the winter. You slept on a flock bed on bed boards and believe me they were hard. Sometimes in winter when it was really cold, the fresh*

If Towage Rate Remain at present Rate of crews
worth on Commission as all other Tugs
Viz
Captain £ 3.10.0 & 5 Per cent on Towage
Engineer £ 3. 5. 0 " " " " on Towage
Fireman £ 2.15.0 " 2½ " "
Mate £ 2.15.0 " 2½ all "

If. Towage. Rate. Increase. 50. Per cent
Captain £ 3.0.0 & 5 Per cent on Towage
Engineer £ 2.15.0 " " "
Fireman £ 2. 5.0 " 2½ " "
Mate £ 2. 5.0 2½ " "

The above Rates at 6 days Per week & Double Pay for Sunday
And if Tugs laid up in for Repairs 10 Shillings Per week
extra all crew And no coaling money to be payed if on
Commission

—————— // ——————

If on a weekly wage at 6 days Per week
Captain £ 5.10.0
Engineer £ 4.10.0
Fireman £ 3.15.0
Mate £ 3.15.0

The working hours Stated in the Terms at
Present issued will be accepted with Double Pay
on Sunday and coaling money to be payed if
on weekly wage

Handwritten list of rates of pay for tug crew. (Laurie Dews)

water in the jug froze. Mind you, the cabins were warm and cosy in winter so long as you kept a nice fire burning.'

Those working on the tugs had a slightly kinder wage structure, but life on the tug boats was just as hard.

'The tugs had a crew of four. The captain and his mate lived in the fore cabin and the engineer and fireman in the aft. This aft cabin led into the engine room and stoke hole. The galley stove was kept burning all night long, with a kettle on top simmering away and the stern gland dripping. That drip, drip, drip could keep a man awake all night!

'The fireman was first up in the morning. He'd walk through the engine room and tunnel into the stoke hole. No time or space for fancy ablutions, just toss it on the fire with a fresh charge of coal to raise steam in the boiler. The engineer would be out of his bed soon after to look after the engine.'

As opposed to the bargemen having to work all hours, the tug's pay rates do take accounts of weekend (double pay on Sundays), allowance for time when laid up for repairs and a degree of commission paid on tonnage; the heavier the load tugged, the more effort needed so the greater the financial reward. The payment system changed in 1948. The captain was now paid £5 5/- (£5.25 or £175 in 2016 values) per week fixed rate and 5d (2p) per ton carried. If the barge was full, that's about £5 per full load or £150 in 2016 values. The annual income for a barge skipper working to this contract would be in the region of £260 fixed rate, and £250 for 50 full loads carried, giving a total of £510. The *Financial Times* figure for average annual earnings in 1948 is £460. A few years later, in 1954, Laurie earned £572.

The post-war settlement showed an improvement in terms and conditions for the bargemen. As the new motorized craft came into the fleet, these conditions improved still further as the physical demands of the job lessened, and the creature comforts on board improved. However the reliance on the state of the river hadn't.

'This wage covered midnight Sunday until midnight Saturday. The only overtime was for cargo loading before 8am or after 5pm or for any work on a Sunday. The mate was also on a weekly wage of £3 and 3d

Laurie's annual pay statements for 1954 and 1971/72. A barge skipper's pay was typical for a skilled working man. Figures from the Financial Times suggest that an average skilled workman's annual pay was in the £550 - £650 range in 1954 and around £2100 in 71/72. Depending on your point of view, Laurie also had the joys or hardship of working in the open air and not being tied to a 9-5 schedule.

(Laurie Dews)

INCOME TAX YEAR 1953-5
CERTIFICATE OF PAY AND TAX DEDUCTED

MR. L. DEWS
(Name of employee as Works No., if any)

Code No. at 5 April, 1954
(Enter "E" if an Emergency
Card is in use at 5.April, 1954.

1. Pay and tax in respect of previous employments) in 1953-54 taken into account arriv at the tax deductions made by me/s

2. **PAY AND TAX IN MY/OUR EMPLOYMENT**

Gross pay			Tax		
£	s.	d.	£		
572	9	5	15	17	

I/We certify that the particulars given above include the total amount of pay (including overtime, bonus, commission, etc.) paid to you by me/us in the year ended 5 April, 1954, and the total tax deducted (less any refunds) in that year.

OLYMPIA MILLS SELBY   21 APR 1954 Date   Employer

TO THE EMPLOYEE. Keep this will help you to check any Notice of Assessment which the tax office ay send you in due course.

YEARLY WAGES 1954

BARGE SELBY TAURUS

BARGE CAPTAINS YEARLY WAGE

FROM MIDNIGHT SUNDAY UNTIL MIDNIGHT SATURDAY

WHICH INCLUDED BASIC WAGE PLUS TONNAGE

ON CARGO CARRIED

DO NOT DESTROY.

CERTIFICATE OF PAY AND TAX DEDUCTED, YEAR 19 **7 1/ 72**

Employer's Name and Address
BOCM SILCOCK LTD.,

Tax District   SELBY

Reference No.

Employee's N.I. No.	Employee's Surname	Inits.	Tax Code	Nature of Employment
	DEWS, L.			

	This Employment			Previous Employment	
Employee's National Ins. Graduated Contributions	Pay	Tax Deducted or Refunded 'R' Indicates Refund 'R'	Pay	Tax Deducted
52.98	1963 83	330.90	.00	.00
	Employee's Superannuation Contributions in this Employment	Holiday Pay Paid but not included above	Total for Year	
			Pay	Tax Deducted
			1963.83	330.90

If Pay and Tax for Wk. 53 inc. above enter		Nett Pay Scheme Only: Gross Pay in this Emp.	
'1'	Pay in Wk. 53	Tax in Wk. 53	

* To the employee. Keep this certificate. It will help you to check any Notice of Assessment that the Tax Office may send you in due course. Failure to produce this form when needed in connection with a claim to National Insurance sickness or unemployment benefit will delay payment of any earnings-related supplement due. A duplicate form P60 cannot be supplied.

I/We certify that the particulars given above include the total amount of pay (including bonus, overtime, commission, etc.) paid to you by me/us in the year ended 5th April last, and the total tax deducted by me/us (less any refunds) in that year.

BOCM SILCOCK LTD.

P 60 (Substitute) (Philips)

(b) The Company shall only give notice at such a time as will ensure for the employee at least a full week's pay from the date of notice and the total notice given shall not at any time be less than that required by any relevant Act of Parliament.

(c) The Company reserves the right to pay wages in lieu of notice.

3. HOURS OF WORK

It is accepted that tidal conditions, the shipping position in the Port of Hull and the supply position of materials at the mill are circumstances which call for a special degree of flexibility in the actual hours worked by crews from day to day.

In recognition of this the Union undertakes that, notwithstanding the definitions which follow of "normal" and "overtime" hours, for the purpose of wage calculations, its members will willingly co-operate in working the craft of which they are the regular crew outside "normal" working hours, to meet the requirements of the Company in relation to the above-mentioned circumstances.

A. "Normal" Hours

(a) The normal working week will be of 40 hours total duration excluding meal times, and shall start at 8 a.m. Monday and finish 5 p.m. Friday.

(b) When not otherwise instructed for operational purposes, attendance shall be from 8 a.m. to 5 p.m. each day, with a one hour meal break taken between 12 noon and 2 p.m. at such time and on such basis as best suits the work situation. Crews will be required to stagger meal breaks as and when necessary and to make such advance preparations to their craft as will enable work to proceed throughout the 2 hour period.

2

B. "Overtime" Hours

(a) With the exception of those special duties noted hereafter under Section 5, all time worked outside "normal" hours will be paid for on the basis specified in the following paragraphs (b) and (c).

(b) "Overtime" worked between 6 a.m. Monday and 6 p.m. Saturday will be paid for at time-and-a-half.

(c) Time worked between 6 p.m. Saturday and 6 a.m. Monday will be paid for at double time.

(d) If, on any occasion, it becomes essential to work through the meal break period of noon—2 p.m., either because the craft is being navigated or because the Company requires it, 1 hour's overtime at the job rate applicable to the work being done and calculated on the basis defined in the preceding paragraphs (b) and (c), will be paid.

4. WAGES

(a) The standard job rate for all classes of Lightermen shall consist of the basic rate for the Seed Crushing, Compound and Provender Manufacturing Industries, as agreed by its National Joint Industrial Council, plus a job premium for navigation as determined under the Company's Job Evaluation Scheme.

(b) This rate shall cover all Lightermen's duties which consist not only of navigating craft, but of loading and discharging both bagged and bulk cargoes, trimming, opening up, covering up, moving and mooring craft, assisting coastwise steamers, towing light craft, eroding berths, standing by, etc.

(c) The Company reserves the right during "normal" hours to detail Lightermen for any type of lighterage work that best suits the work situation, whether or not normally carried out by Lightermen prior to this time, and to nominate temporary substitutes as Captains or Mates for any craft.

3

---

per ton. You were expected to live on board all week. If you lived in Selby and the boat was in Hull, or vice versa you received one rail fare to go home at weekends and return Monday morning.'

Extract from book of terms and conditions for workers on the river, 1966.

(Laurie Dews)

The bargemen remained careful with their money. Many more people smoked back in the 1950s, and it was essential to make those cigarettes last as long as possible.

'We used to save up our tab ends and mix them with dried tea leaves and put them all in a jar. If we were fog bound and didn't have any cigs we'd break open the jar and roll up the tobacco and tea leaves into cigarettes to have a smoke.'

A decade later, rates of pay and terms and conditions were agreed in negotiations between management and unions, with rights and responsibilities clearly laid out.

Section 6 also shows that by 1966, the company had decided to supply coal at a moderate rate per month to save the need for

(e) **Early Morning Tidesman.** The following payment will apply:—

4 hours (plain time) at standard job rate when reporting time is before 6 a.m.

2 hours (plain time) at standard job rate when reporting time is after 6 a.m. and before 8 a.m.

(f) **Missed Navigation.** When *crews report* and navigation is cancelled due to weather conditions the following payments will be made:—

3 hours (plain time) at standard job rate when reporting time is before 5 a.m.

2 hours (plain time) at standard job rate when reporting time is after 5 a.m. and before 8 a.m.

(g) **Delays en Route.** Crews required to stand by craft necessarily delayed en route by weather conditions, engine failure, etc., will be paid at their standard job rate and on the appropriate overtime basis for all "overtime" involved during the first twenty-four hours after departure.

Thereafter and until navigation is resumed, waiting time only will be paid at the N.J.I.C. basic rate (plain time) for all "overtime" hours involved between 6 a.m. Monday and midnight Friday, at time-and-a-half between midnight Friday and 6 p.m. Saturday and at double time between 6 p.m. Saturday and 6 a.m. Monday.

(h) **Weekends.** Lightermen ordered in and who report for work between Saturday midnight and Sunday midnight shall be paid not less than 4 hours (double time) at the job rate for the work they expected to do.

(i) **Weekend Pumpmen.** The following payments will be made at the special rate applicable:—

Hull: 3 hours at time-and-a-half for one Saturday visit.

3 hours at double time for one Sunday visit.

6

Selby: 2 hours at time-and-a-half for each Saturday visit before 6 p.m.

2 hours at double time for a Saturday visit later than 6 p.m.

2 hours at double time for each of two Sunday visits.

(j) **Aeger Watch.** Lightermen specially called in on overtime for this duty will be paid 2 hours at the rate applicable and on the appropriate overtime basis.

(k) **Towing Rate.** Power craft towing light dumb craft, B.O.C.M. owned or hired craft,

One lighter on tow—1½ hours (plain time) JOB RATE
Two lighters on tow—3 hours (plain time)

This payment will be applied to both members of the powered craft at their own respective standard job rates for journeys from:—

Selby, Howdendyke, Goole, Cato II or H.O.M.C.O. Mills to the Hull Docks.

No payments for tows other than the above will be made.

(l) **Painting.** Crews will be required to paint the craft to which they are attached, once per year. For this the following bonus will be paid:—

Powered Craft: 40 hours (plain time) at the N.J.I.C. basic rate to be shared pro rata amongst those participating.

Dumb Craft: 32 hours „ „ „ „ „
To be payable on request after satisfactory completion.

6. **COAL**

Coal for use on Olympia lighters will be supplied by the Company on the basis of a maximum of one cwt. per

7

A second extract from book of terms and conditions for workers on the river, 1966. (Laurie Dews)

thievery. BOCM's continued use of the barge fleet on the river was subject to annual agreement by the City of York Corporation, who, at the time, were the authority in control of the river from York to Hook railway bridge.

Note that, although the motor vessels were designed to work independently, they could also act as tugs for the remaining dumb barges should the amount of cargo to be moved require it. BOCM kept up this contract on Laurie's barge, the *Selby Michael* until at least 1983, although regular use had ceased some eighteen months earlier.

Chapter 13

RETIREMENT

I n the mid-1960s, eight barges were unloading daily at Barlby. If each barge delivered their full capacity, that was around 2,000 tons of seed. As most lorries of the time had a capacity less than twenty tons, that meant that eight barges shifted the equivalent of over 100 lorry journeys. Whilst the road journey between Hull and Selby on the A63 might only take a quarter of the time that a barge would need on the river, each lorry had less than a tenth of the capacity. To use lorries to deliver an equivalent tonnage of cargo would also require about ten times the workforce, with all the extra cost that would imply. River transport still had a clear advantage.

Unfortunately, three key developments did away with that edge over the ensuing twenty years. Rotterdam replaced Hull as the major port for ocean-going freighters bringing loads from Africa. Cargoes were often trans-shipped there, meaning that coasters could by-pass Hull to deliver as far inland as Goole or even to the riverside jetties in Selby. Barges could still collect from these wharves and take the seed to Barlby, but the advantage in using a slow, bulk-carrying mode of transport such as a barge is lessened when deliveries take place over shorter distances, and more intermittently. Fewer barges travelled along the river, and more lorries were serviced at the Ousegate wharves in Selby, where seed was unloaded and taken the brief, two-mile trip over the Toll Bridge to the Barlby works.

The design of lorries themselves was steadily improved to cater for larger capacities. Alongside the growing motorway network, these changes meant that bulk road transport became more rapid and economic. One barge's load was now only equivalent to six lorries-worth, and road collection and delivery from Goole took less than an hour, many times quicker than by barge.

Increased canal tolls and dock charges further eroded the cost advantages of water transport. Although the license for an HGV was expensive, that was a one-off, annual charge. Tolls, wharfage and handling costs were incurred for every shipment.

On top of that, only one man was needed to drive a lorry, and with the reduction in demarcation in handling cargoes, using road transport required less manpower, meaning the firm's wage costs were reduced.

All these factors meant that as the 1970s wore on, the decision that BOCM had to make about whether to renew their barge fleet or not tipped away from the use of the river. Signs of demise at Selby were becoming apparent. Michael Pearson, writing in *Waterways World* in November 1980 observed the decay of physical resources and the loss of age-old skills:

'… we've been using the Ouse since Roman times, but for how much longer? Shipping to Selby is safe and growing … but BOCM's fleet and men … are ageing and need new investment'.

In the same article, Laurie commented, *'a vessel of some sort could be built for road trailers and lorries to drive on and off a barge with no need for transhipping'*. Universal containerization which is commonplace in 2016 was a dream in 1980, as was the change in the working world needed to enable it. Michael Pearson could see the strength in Laurie's idea but wondered 'whether he'd get that idea past the Hull dockers'. The thought that unionised labour could successfully hope to resist such modernization seems as odd now as the concept of container ships must have done then. Whilst all these changes were going on in the background, Laurie introduced his family to the joys

Laurie's son Richard, probably aboard the *Selby Michael*.
(Laurie Dews)

of the waterways. Just as Sam had shown Laurie the ropes on board, Laurie himself took eldest son Raymond on the *Selby Castor* a few times.

'My two nieces Maureen and Susan had a ride up to Selby on the Castor *when they were staying with their grandma in Hull. They said they'd loved every minute. Now they're older with their own families they talk and laugh about this "cruise". By the time younger son Richard was old enough to come on board, I was skipper of the* Selby Michael, *and we had a few trips on board to Hull and Gainsborough. When we were moored up, he liked to go fishing in the docks.'*

Laurie and Richard in the cabin of the *Selby Michael.*
(Laurie Dews)

However much fun these trips were, neither Raymond nor Richard took up a life afloat, instead settling for careers in engineering. Had they even wanted to follow in the family footsteps, the changes in the freight universe made such a course impossible. The inevitable decision to cease river

Laurie's son Richard and friends in the wheelhouse of a motorized barge.
(Laurie Dews)

Selby Maurice, Selby Richard (in front), *Selby Michael* and *Selby Phillipa* (behind) – potentially used as floating storage, but seemingly abandoned on the river bank, along with another member of the fleet, at Barlby in 1997.

(Laurie Dews)

transport came in the early 1980s. The barges that had served BOCM well for twenty years or so were pensioned off. Selby crews were made redundant in October 1981, with Hull men following a year later. The final seed cargo moved by members of the fleet occurred in 1982 when a load of shea nuts were brought to Selby from Goole. After this the craft were moored on the Ouse by the mills at Barlby for use as storage.

The 1990s saw the craft gradually sold off. *Ellen* and *Linda* were leased then presumably purchased by Humber Barges for aggregate work on the Trent and to Leeds. More went entirely to the Trent to be used by Mason Brothers around Gainsborough and Newark and Waddington's at Swinton purchased six. Others remained available for private sale or community use. As for Laurie, after the boats were moored up for the final time, he was employed by BOCM mainly on land-based work, as well as acting as a river pilot for skippers who did not have a working knowledge of the wiles of the Ouse.

One of Laurie's last jobs was loading a cargo of oil drums using the crane on the wharf. This veteran crane, dating from

A Crane built Taylor and Hubbard of Leicester's crane on the jetty at Barlby in 2010, around 20 years after its final use. (Author)

the early years of the factory, didn't have a sufficiently long jib to place the oil drums in the barge's hold.

'We couldn't get close enough to the jetty, so the bloke working the crane had to get the net of oil drums swinging. When the net swung out towards the barge, he released it and the drums flew into the hold. By, they made a noise!'

River trade continued to decline, and the retirement age of 65 loomed.

'The time came for me to retire on 19 September 1987 after fifty years of working the river. In all that time, I'd only fallen overboard twice. Once was in summer, but the worst one was in winter when there were ice floes in the river. A rope slipped and knocked me in. When the crew pulled me back on board I was never so cold in my whole life. What with the wind whistling through my sodden clothes, it was like standing there with nothing on! The rum came in handy again – it was the best medicine!

'Anyway, the managing director called me into the office, gave me a large cheque, assured me of a monthly pension and wished me all the best for my retirement. In some ways, I'd done much better with a pension than my dad Sam. When he retired in 1953 he got a lump sum of £900 (about £25,000 today), but no weekly pension – and he lived another twenty-seven years

'I had a lot of hard times on the river, but also a lot of good times. The job taught you how to look after yourself and learn lots of skills like painting, rope work and cooking. I made many friends, but I hardly see them now as they nearly all lived in and around Hull.'

Over the years since Laurie's retirement, the former BOCM site has gradually fallen into disrepair and dereliction. The old factory buildings are gradually being demolished. There are plans for 'Olympia Park' – a development of new houses, shops and light industry, with the former works' clock tower as a central feature, but at the time of writing in early 2016, little constructive work appears to have been done on the site.

'It was sad to look back on things after I retired. I had the chance to come down river from York on a pleasure boat, the River Palace *after I'd retired. As we passed the BOCM jetties at Selby, I saw all their motor boats moored up, rusting away and thought what a shame that was. They could still have been put to use transporting cargoes. A few were initially used for storage, some were sold off as house boats but most were broken up. These conversions are worth a lot of money. One – either the* Richard *or the* Doris *– has been recently advertised for sale at £200,000!'*

Even after retirement, the river continues to hold a fascination.

As described in chapter 1, the Norse-named river wave, the aegir, shows the tidal nature of the Ouse. Many people have heard of the River Severn's bore, and perhaps have seen pictures of foolhardy folk surfing on it through Gloucestershire. The Ouse's aegir isn't surfable, but at full and new moons, particularly around spring and autumn equinoxes, the wave is an eerily wonderful natural phenomenon to observe.

When Selby had trade that depended on the river, most families knew about for the aegir and looked out for it. Now that the town has turned its back on the river, it has become a little known experience. Laurie took great delight in introducing his grandchildren to this minor wonder of nature.

'They used to say to me, "Granddad – what's this river wave?" I took them down to the river bank just downstream from Selby Toll Bridge. We got comfy and watched the river flow. After ten minutes or so, they were getting bored and wanted to go home.

'But I told them to wait – then suddenly the river current stilled, and we could hear a whooshing in the distance like a flock of birds swooping overhead. Then we saw the reeds moving and then there it was – nine waves, one after the other, thrusting upstream, carrying all kinds of debris. The children looked on amazed. Their quiet river had changed into a torrent flowing in the opposite direction, and the level had gone up so much we had to move up the bank so as not to get our feet wet.'

The training walls at Trent Falls have reduced the power of the aegir, but when the shipyards were still in business, on the appropriate days, a lookout was posted to cry out 'Wor ! Aegir!' and the men working on the ships would rapidly gather up their tools and move up the bank. They didn't want their belongings swept up along with the general debris. One of the

Selby Tony being pushed upriver through Selby Rail bridge, 2016. (Author)

Selby Tony passing the remains of the Barlby wharves, 2016. (Author)

fleet did make a brief return to Selby over thirty years since being in regular traffic. The *Selby Tony* had been rescued from dereliction, renovated and made watertight, to be hauled to a mooring in York where it is planned it will become an arts venue called the York Artsbarge. Its dimensions of approximately 100x20 feet will be put to good use in providing a performance space, art gallery, bar and meeting rooms. The hulk was pushed upriver through Selby in March 2016.

The convoy also passed the *Tony*'s old work haunts at the BOCM jetties. The dereliction at this site is clear to see.

'*Another sad moment was dealing with the death of my parents. Before my Dad died at the age of 91 in 1980 he had told me that he wanted his ashes scattering on the river. One morning about 5am I was on the* Michael *between the Humber Bridge and buoy 28A. I slowed the engine down, and Johnny Roddam who was mate with me, came up on deck, doffed his cap and bowed his head as I scattered my dad's ashes over the stern.*

'*Seven years later Mother died. Elisabeth had always been one for a challenge. Even at the age of 90, when she was in a wheelchair, she* had a lot of spirit. She took part in a sponsored glider trip over the Humber Bridge. Now the glider had two compartments – one at the front for the passenger, and the one behind for the pilot. Mam didn't know this, so when we put her into the front cockpit, she shouted out in alarm, "Am I supposed to fly this? You know I've never flown a glider before!" Reassured by the arrival of the real pilot, she had a great time and helped to raise a lot of money for Selby War Memorial Hospital.

Remains of a wharf at Selby, 2014. (Author)

'She had wanted me to spread her ashes as I had done with Dad, but by then I had retired, so had no boat. Instead my wife Marian and I drove down to the Humber Bridge. I waded out as far as I could and put her ashes on the water.'

As for Laurie himself, he seems to have summed it up nicely when he spoke to a group of boating enthusiasts in Cottingham, near Hull in 2014.

Derelict state of the wharf at Barlby, 2014. (Author)

'I can't complain. I've had a pretty good life. On the barges I never had to clock on, never had to work nine to five and worked with a great bunch of lads in a job I'd always wanted to do. You can't do much better than that.'

As for the Selby Waterfront, the Barlby factory and the fleet of BOCM barges, they still exist in one form or another, albeit greatly changed from Laurie's time.

The wharves that lined Ousegate in Selby lay unused for many years from the mid-1990s. Wintertime high river levels have washed away much that remained of the wooden structures of the wharves and jetties. Once it was finally decided that there was no commercial future for Williamson's wharf, a small-scale housing development

Part of the BOCM
factory being
demolished, 2016.
(Author)

Derelict part of
the BOCM factory
complex 2013.
(Author)

was begun there in 2015. The railway wharf remains empty and unused. Flats were built on the site of Connell's yard in 2004, and the Sturge and Tate and Lyle jetties fell into disuse before that. Cochrane's shipyard closed in the early 1990s with large areas of the site still remaining derelict.

Large swathes of the BOCM factory now lie either derelict or cleared to allow for the new developments. The wharves and jetties – subject to an improvement grant as recently as 2000 – are now in a ruinous state, with the historic Taylor and Hubbard crane that still remains on the wharf being in danger of toppling into the river. (Page 165.)

Perhaps most poignantly, Laurie's old barge, the *Selby Michael* remains afloat and on a river that she once served commercially, being tied up at Hazleford Lock, on the Trent. Sadly, she does not seem to be moored in any positive or meaningful fashion, having apparently been abandoned there since spring 2015. As the accompanying photos taken in March 2016 sadly show, she is slowly rusting away, her hold gradually filling with flood water and general debris. The carrying capacity of the hold remains clear to see. Even in this state, when photographed from a friendly angle, and using poetic licence aided by a tear in the eye, one can still imagine, fifty-six years after launch, *Michael* proudly awaiting to proceed down river carrying out a centuries-old commercial purpose, with her skipper cheerfully and confidently in command.

Remnants of the overhead railway, facing onto Barlby Road, 2014. (Author)

Retired barge skipper and lighterman, Laurie Dews, 2014. The cheery grin and jauntily-angled cap remain constant . Look again at the picture from some seventy-five years earlier, on page 63. (Author)

Selby Michael tied up at Hazleford Lock on the Trent, 2016. (Author)

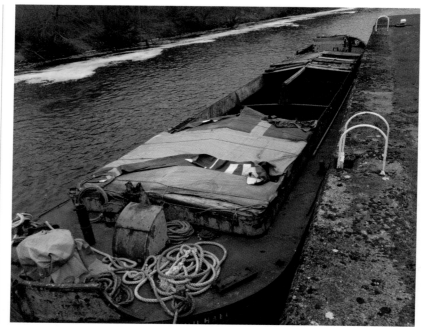

Selby Michael, as moored at Hazleford Lock, 2016, showing the capacity of the cargo hold. (Author)

THE OCO/BOCM BARGE FLEETS

This is a table of Watson's original craft, barges of approximately 97ft by 18ft, to carry 200 tons of cargo. An * next to the name of a Selby barge means it remained part of the BOCM fleet in 1980, having given over fifty years' service.

Place name	Cosmic Name	Built at	Build date	Skippers (where known)	Notes
Leeds	Aurora	Hessle	1910	G. Wilson	
Leeds	Axis	Hessle	1911	T. Crossland	
Leeds	Comet	Howdendyke	1909	G. Middleton	
Leeds	Eclipse	Howdendyke	1910	E. Holdgate	
Leeds	Jupiter	Beverley	1910	N.Taylor	
Leeds	Luminary	Howdendyke	1911		
Leeds	Magnetic	Beverley	1910	T. Greaves	Still working around York in 1979
Leeds	Mars	Beverley	1909	J. Chambers	
Leeds	Mercury	Beverley	1909	A. Crossland	
Leeds	Meteor	Hessle	1910	R. Wray	
Leeds	Neptune	Hessle	1909	T. Dews	Laurie's Uncle Tommy
Leeds	Orbit	Hessle	1910	J. Ward	
Leeds	Planet	Hessle	1910	J. Gledhall	
Leeds	Polar	Beverley	1910	J. Wray	
Leeds	Radius	Beverley	1911	J. Middleton	
Leeds	Satellite	Hessle	1910	A. Close	
Leeds	Saturn	Beverley	1910	D. Hall	
Leeds	Solar	Hessle	1910	T. Holdgate	
Leeds	Uranus	Hessle	1909	A. Taylor	Destroyed in Hull Docks in Second World War
Leeds	Venus	Beverley	1910	W. Gillyon	
Leeds	Vulcan	Beverley	1911	J. Calvert	
Selby	Andromeda *	Thorne	1922	F. Markham	
Selby	Argo *	Thorne	1921	J. Dyson	
Selby	Capella *	Hessle	1921	H. Wray	
Selby	Castor *	Beverley	1915	A. Wray	Dual purpose - tanker or dry goods
Selby	Cygnus	Hessle	1921	G. Lawrence	
Selby	Draco *	Hessle	1921	J. Gillyon	
Selby	Leo *	Hessle	1921	F. Leegus	
Selby	Lyra	Beverley	1915	R. Taylor	Dual purpose - tanker or dry goods
Selby	Orion	Hessle	1921	W. Foster	
Selby	Pollux	Beverley	1915	C. Ward	Dual purpose - tanker or dry goods
Selby	Sirius	Thorne	1921	F. Holdgate	Used for barrage balloons in the Humber
Selby	**Taurus**	**Thorne**	**1921**	**S. Dews**	**Laurie's dad's boat**
Selby	Vega	Beverley	1915	G. Dyson	Dual purpose - tanker or dry goods
Selby	Virgo *	Thorne	1921	A. Dews	Laurie's Great Uncle Abe (63 in 1937)

Laurie, his grand-daughter Gail and 3 other BOCM bargemen aboard the 'Selby Michael' at Whitaker's Dry Dock in Hull, circa 1980.

Standard maintenance was at Connell's Yard and Dry Dock, next to Selby Lock, at the junction of the Ouse and the Selby Canal.

Several families had more than one barge. Not only were the Dews family heavily involved with Watsons, but the Wrays, Dysons, Taylors, Holdgates and the Middletons were also families with strong links to the Selby barge trade.

These barges were built to last. Some were commandeered for use by the war department around Hull in the Second World War. Others may have been sunk in accidents (*Selby Pollux*) or burnt out by incendiaries (*Selby Taurus*) but in many cases they were repaired at the dry docks in Hull and gave over thirty years of service before being replaced by the motorized barges in the 1950s. By the end of the 1950s, the BOCM fleet had been modernized and consisted of eighteen self-propelled craft and nine remaining dumb barges.

With the return of the barge skippers from the Second World War, and the introduction of the motorized barges in the table on page 175 in the 1950s, there were naturally changes in the roster. These are the details of the skippers as Laurie remembers them, from 1969 and 1980.

Name of craft (all prefixed *Selby*)	Skipper in 1969	Skipper in 1980	Carrying Capacity (Tons)	Year built at Thorne	Engine type and Motive power (Horsepower)	Notes
Charles	Charlie Ward	S. Wilcockson	250	1957	Gardner 95	
Corrie	Ken Simpson		200	1955	Lister 62	
Doris	Stan Wilcox		200	1954	Lister 60	
Elizabeth	John Middleton	Harold Shires	250	1959	Gardner 95	
Ellen	Jim Taylor		250	1954	Gardner 110	Engine uprated from 60 hp
Janet	Harold Wray	Harold Wray	250	1957	Gardner 95	
Judith	R. Robinson	D. Hardy	250	1957	Gardner 95	
Linda	George Beevers		250	1954	Gardner 110	Engine uprated from 60 hp
Margaret	Ted Taylor	Ted Taylor	250	1962	Gardner 110	
Martin	Bill Dyson	K. Simpson	250	1959	Gardner 95	
Maurice	Wally Batty	Johnny Roddam	250	1962	Gardner 110	
Michael	Laurie Dews	Laurie Dews	250	1960	Gardner 95	
Peter	Les Taylor	Les Taylor	250	1955	Gardner 110	Engine uprated from 60 hp
Philippa	Ron Swatman		200	1955	Lister 62	
Richard	C. Wilkinson		200	1954	Lister 62	
Robin	Tom Metcalf	T. Malcolm	250	1955	Gardner 110	Engine uprated from 60 hp
Sara	Albert Wray	R. Johnson	250	1960	Gardner 95	
Tony	Johnny Roddam	K. Shires	250	1957	Gardner 95	

A presentation to BOCM skippers and their wives c. 1961, to mark 15 years of service. L to R (rear) L. Taylor; E Taylor; Mrs. E. Taylor; L. Dews; H. Wray; Mrs. H. Wray and W. Batty (front) Mrs. L. Taylor; Mr. Flohil; Mrs. L. Dews and Mrs. W. Batty. Mr. Flohil was the chairman at BOCM who decided to give the fleet of motorized barges their personal names.

The barges were given individual names linked to those of the family of the general manager of BOCM at the time, a Mr Flohill, or of families who worked in the BOCM offices.

Not all of the barges had electric light initially, and all were without radar. After Connell's dry dock in Selby closed in the late 1950s, maintenance switched to the Yorkshire Dry Dock Company in Hull. By 1969, some of the earlier barges with less powerful engines had begun to be phased out, marking the beginning of the end of the BOCM river traffic. Some nine dumb barges also remained in service and two more steel barges were added from Dunston's yard in 1952, the *Selby Libra* and the *Selby Capricorn*. By 1980, if they were still with BOCM, they were probably used as merely static storage vessels.

Some of the family names from the 1920s were still in evidence – not only Dews, but also Taylor, Wray and Middleton.

The City of York Corporation were responsible for the River Ouse navigation from York to Hook Railway Bridge. From the time they gained that responsibility in 1879, they provided a public towing service between York, Selby, Goole and Hull.

By 1920, five tugs were available for this service.
- *Ebor Express*: 1878–1930. Her name board is preserved at the buildings at Naburn Lock.
- *City of York*: 1888–1923. Ended up in Hull as a coal boat.
- *Lancelot*: 1905–1947. Sold to Peter Foster to tow barges in Hull.
- *Sir Joseph Rymer*: 1909–1937.
- *Robie*: 1915–1924. She is said to have been one of the tugs that led the German Fleet into Scapa Flow in 1918 at the end of the First World War.

The engineer was a chap called Walter Press from Fulford near York. He and *Robie* must clearly have had a poor time at Scapa as the following letter from the river Navigation offices at Naburn, dated February 1919, has Walter in hospital in Scotland and *Robie* yet to be 'released' (presumably from war service). In fact, hauling on the Ouse in early 1919 must have been in a bad way as the letter describes ailments of other members of the fleet.

The tug *Robie*, one of the mainstays of BOCM's river-based transport. (Laurie Dews)

The Ouse Navigation Trustees, owners of the Steam Tugs "City of York," "Ebor Express," "Robie," "Lancelot," and "Sir Joseph Rymer," HEREBY GIVE NOTICE that they will tow Vessels, Boats or other Craft, by the above-named Steam Tugs, or other Steam Tugs, on the following Conditions only, viz.:—

That the Trustees are not to be held to give any warranty, either implied or otherwise, that their Tugs are capable of performing any work undertaken by them.

That they are not to be answerable or accountable for any loss, including loss of life or damage whatever, which may happen to or be occasioned by any of the above-named Steam Tugs, or any persons on board the same, or to or by any Vessel, Boat, or Craft, or any Persons or Cargoes on board the same, whilst such Vessel, Boat, or Craft is in tow of any of the above-named Steam Tugs, whether arising from or occasioned by any alleged breach of warranty or implied term of the towage contract, or any alleged negligence or default of them or their servants, or from or by insufficient towing power, or any other defect or imperfection of any kind whatever in the said Steam Tugs or any of them, or the machinery or any other part of the same, or from or by any delay, stoppage, or slackness of the speed of the same, however occasioned, or for what purpose soever, or wheresoever taking place.

And that the owner or persons interested in the Vessels, Boats, or Craft, or the Cargoes on board the same, or any of them, so being towed undertake to bear, satisfy, indemnify and save harmless the said Trustees against all or any such loss or damage and all liability for the same, and against all costs and charges in respect of any law expenses or actions that may arise or be brought against the said Trustees in relation to any such loss or damage actual or alleged.

Terms—Cash.

TELEGRAMS:
GUILDHALL, YORK.
TELEPHONE NO. 70.

J. S. MUMMERY,
RIVER MANAGER.

The Ouse Navigation Offices,

Naburn Locks,

York Feby. 28th 1919.

Mr. W. W. Press,
A.1. Ward,
R.N. Hospital,
LARBERT,
Stirlingshire.

Dear Sir,

I am in receipt of your letter and I am pleased to hear that you are progressing favourably. I was sorry to hear from Captain Young that you were so ill, I am pleased Mrs. Press has been with you, and I hope you have been well looked after in the Hospital. You seem to have had a very bad time, but now that you have got a change for the better I hope you will soon be well again.

So far as I know, things are going on alright on board the "Robie". I understand that Drust is acting as engineer and that they have got another fireman.

I have no news of the "Lancelot" or the "Robie" being released as yet. The "City of York" has been laid at Hull nearly three months waiting for 7 new stays in the boiler and a new crank shaft for the port engine. The long delay is on account of the strike.

Young Amos Camplejohn has left us and gone to work at the Ardol Mills, Richardson has been demobilized and he has also gone to the Ardol Mills. S. Hall, temporary captain of the "Ebor Express" went home ill last November and has not been to work since. J.Wright has been demobilized and takes up his former duties as captain of the "Ebor Express" to-day.

We are still struggling on at the Locks, I hope in the course of a few more weeks that we shall get back again to something like normal times.

Yours faithfully,

Jas. B. Mummery

Letter of 1919 to Mr Prest concerning the state of the *Robie* and the other Ouse tugs. (Laurie Dews)

Robie went on to work on the Ouse until scrappage in the 1950s.

These tugs were coal-powered steam tugs, and normally had their bunkers filled at the railway jetty in Selby, from coal wagons proceeding directly across Ousegate from the goods station.

Another tug, of unknown dates was the *Enterprise*. She became the fire barge in York. In the 1920s, Whitaker's of Hull took over some of the towing duties and OCO provided their own tugs, one of which was the *Robie*.

Following decommissioning of the fleet by BOCM, the eighteen motorised barges of the fleet have enjoyed various fates. As of May 2016, I understand these fates to be as follows:

Barge	Reported fate
Charles	
Corrie	
Doris	Possibly at Yorkshire Waterways Museum, Goole
Elizabeth	
Ellen	At Hermitage Community Moorings, Wapping, London, 2015
Janet	Seen in the livery of another company at wharves possibly in Nottingham in 1999
Judith	Tied up on River Hull by former BOCM works, 2004
Linda	Carrying aggregate for Humber Barges to Leeds in 1999 (along with *Selby Ellen*, both being 'leased' from BOCM)
Margaret	Reported as 'in London' in 2011
Martin	Waddington's boatyard/scrap line Swinton, 2008
Maurice	Privately owned, moored in London, 2009
Michael	Reported tied up and disused in Nottingham, 2009. Moored at Hazleford Weir near Newark, 2015. Still there in March 2016
Peter	Awaiting scrapping at Waddington's yard, 2013
Philippa	Possibly at Yorkshire Waterways Museum, Goole
Richard	Possibly in Canary Wharf, London, 2015, offered for sale at £375,000 as converted to a houseboat. Painted in colours of 'Flixborough Shipping'
Robin	Reported in December 2012 as 'laying in Yorkshire' and available for sale for £50,000 - 'can be cut and shut to your requirements'
Sara	
Tony	Hulk made watertight at Waddington's, 2015. Taken up to be moored on the Foss at York to become the 'York Artsbarge'

Following the Second World War, two diesel-powered 'TID's were purchased for towing duties. These had been originally built for the war effort between 1943 and 1946. 'TID' might be an acronym for 'Tug: Inshore and Dock', although it is said that due to their work in readiness for D-Day, it stood for 'Tug Invasion Duty'. They were 70 feet long, with a pulling power of

Former TID, now BOCM tug *OCO*, having sunk at Swinefleet, January 1961. (Laurie Dews)

just over 200 horsepower. Most of the vessels were built by Dunston's at Thorne, and due to wartime demands they were made to a tight schedule and to a simplified design. It was stated that the Admiralty required *'one tug per week, using in the process little or no shipyard labour'*. The vessels were rapidly constructed from prefabricated sections supplied to the yard.

'Spike Wadsworth told me those TIDs were death traps. A proper tug needs a rounded hull, so if she starts to list to one side the curve of the hull will right her. But the TIDs had angled hulls. So as soon as they started to list there was nothing to stop them and they'd roll right over.'

This was quite possibly the cause of the sinking of the *OCO* in 1961.

The tug *OCO* was originally TID 118 and part of the Navy's active fleet in 1944/45. It was planned that she would be fitted out for 'tropical work' in the Far East, but instead was sold to the mill in 1947. When refloated after the 1961 incident, she was renamed *Selby Olympia*. The tug *Ardol* was originally TID 77, and came to the company in 1950. She was broken up at Paull on the Humber in 1960.

In the early days of the mill, there were also two wooden barges, the *Thermagene* and *Thermastat*. They were both oil tankers and were taken out of service around 1938.

MAKING YOUR OWN ENTERTAINMENT

As was the case with many manual workers, Laurie and the bunch of bargemen in and around Hull Docks had plenty of songs they could sing whilst having a mash of tea together.

'Back then we didn't have a radio or anything like that – but we got together and made our own amusement. One bloke'd have a mouth organ, maybe another with a Jew's harp and everyone else would stamp their feet to get the rhythm and we'd have a good sing-song.'

Here are five songs that Laurie still croons, and as you might expect, they are a mix of lyrics from the folk tradition and more modern musical-hall type songs. There were also songs from the military tradition from when many of the bargemen were signed up to work on landing craft. Laurie talks about some of the songs being from a 'sod's opera' – where some of the squaddies cross-dressed in the panto tradition.

1. *Big Strong Man or My Brother Sylveste*

This song with Irish connections is well known in folk circles. The reference to having 'lived in a caravan' might link to the Irish Traveller community, well-known for both bare-knuckle and professional (gloved) boxers. It was also a song that was sung in the music halls.

> Have you heard about the big strong man?
> He lives in a caravan
> He plays the organ in the belfry
> And he wants to fight Jack Dempsey
>
> CHORUS

O that's my brother Sylvest (shout - What's he got?)
He's got a row of forty medals on his chest (shout - Big Chest!)
He fought the forty darkies in the west
He takes no rest, think of a man,
Hells fire, son of a gun
Don't push, just shove, plenty of room for me and you.
He's got an arm like a leg (shout - a lady's leg!)
And a punch that'll sink a battle ship (shout - Big Ship!)
It takes all the army and the navy to put the wind up Sylveste

O he thought he'd take a trip by the sea
So he took himself a trip to New York
he jumped in the harbour in New York
and swam like a man made of Cork

CHORUS

He saw the good ship *Lusitania* in distress (What'd he do?)
He swallowed all the water in the sea (big swallow!)
He put the Lusitania on his chest (big chest!)
And took the lot to Italy

CHORUS

Well he thought he'd take a trip to old Japan
And they turned out the whole big brass band
He played every instrument they had
He broke the whole darn lot

CHORUS

References to early twentieth century cultural heroes place the hey-day of the song a little before the time Laurie started on the barges in the 1930s. The RMS *Lusitania* was a British-built ocean liner, launched in 1906 for Cunard. She held the Blue Riband for the fastest maritime crossing of the Atlantic. She was sunk after an infamous torpedo attack in 1915, killing almost 1,200 passengers and crew.

Jack Dempsey was World Heavyweight Champion from 1919–26, famed for the power of his punching. Originally named William, he changed his name to Jack as a tribute to an Irish fighter of that name from an earlier generation.

As with all songs like this, they are remembered slightly differently. Other published versions talk about a fight with Jack Johnson – another hard-punching heavyweight champ a little before Dempsey. In the last line, some versions replace 'wind up Sylveste' with the cheekier 'bra off Mae West'; Mae West, being a femme fatale from the 1920s, famous for the invitation to 'come up and see me some time'.

Sometimes there are not forty but fifty medals on his chest, and a wide variety of foes are fought 'in the west'.

The song remains active in the folk tradition. Little and Large included their version in a stage show and on a 1990s album. There is even a racehorse that shares the name of the song! A recent version changes the boxer reference to George Foreman, with the couplet

'He used to work here as a doorman
Now he wants to fight George Foreman'

The Tyson Fury version can't be far off!

2. *Drury Lane*

When I was just a parlourmaid down in Drury Lane
Oh the mistress was so kind to me and the master was the same
Till up came a sailor boy just got home from sea
And that was the start of my misery

He asked for a candle to light his way to bed
And he asked for a pillow to rest his weary head
Now silly girl me not thinking it no harm
I jumped into bed just to keep that sailor warm

Early next morning, the sailor he arose
And pulled out his pocket a five pound note
Take that my darling for the damage I have done
I'm leaving you in charge of a daughter or a son

If it be a daughter then bounce her on your knee
And if it be a son send the young lad off to sea

With bell bottom trousers and a suit of navy blue
Just let him climb the rigging as all sailors do

Now take a tip you parlour maids - and take a tip from me
Never let a sailor get an inch above your knee
For if you do he will never never stop
Till he's climbing up the rigging to the old crows' nest

Laurie freely adapts the old song *Rosemary Lane,* a folk song dating back to around 1810.

According to Roud & Bishop in their *New Penguin Book of Folk Songs* it is:

'An extremely widespread song, in Britain and America. Its potential for bawdy means that it was popular in male-centred contexts such as rugby clubs, army barracks and particularly in the navy, where it can still be heard, but traditional versions were often collected from women as well as men.'

Although Laurie doesn't sing it to this tune, it does fit *Rock-a-Bye Baby.* I've recorded the last line as Laurie sang it, but a substitution of something like 'until he reaches to the top' would rhyme and still be a suitable double entendre, although missing out on the nautical reference to a crow's nest lookout. The song was recorded in 1969 by well-known folk singer Bert Jansch, and is also apparently the marching song of the United States Army 10th Mountain Division where the lyrics are altered to tell the young lad to go 'off to ski'.

The song is also known as *Bell Bottom Trousers* – a reference to the flared service trousers worn by sailors. The sum of money changes with the times, and the young lad is often appropriately referred to as a 'bastard'.

3. *Dujardin's Navy*
This was sung to the tune of *John Brown's Body.*

We are the jolly lighter lads, the lighter lads are we
We do not sail the ocean and we don't go down to sea
We are the jolly lighter lads of SW&T
In Dujardin's navy

When we're towing out the lock. our vessel's shipped to sea
The icy cold water comes swimming round about our knees
When we're towed by Riverside Quay we cannot see the clock
In Dujardin's Navy

We have ourselves a skipper in the job, his name is Joseph Plug
He wasn't going fast enough so he bought himself a tug
Now he doing two trips a week and most of them are snug
In Dujardin's Navy

'SW&T' stood for Selby Warehousing and Transport, a subsidiary part of the OCO enterprise, the early name for Watson's barge fleet, and Mr Dujardin was the General Manager in Selby around the turn of the 1930s.

It would be implausibly quick to make two trips a week, but if you could, it would make the skipper a good profit. Joseph Plug was the nickname for one of the barge skippers who was keen to make as much money as possible.

'That skipper was always after cargoes that weighed heavy like linseed, ground nuts, maize, barley or palm kernels. We called these running seed because they filled the cargo space easily and fitted nicely under the hatches. Cargoes like Copra, locust bean, cotton seed or material in sacks was more trouble and took more time to load and unload. These cargoes weighed light so we had to put on pestering boards inside the combings to make the hold higher to take more cargo.'

The clock tower was built on the south side of Albert Dock with a clock face on either side. Damaged in the Hull Blitz, it was demolished after the war.

4. *Maggie May*
Oh well do I recall
When I first met Maggie May
Cruising up and down old Canning Place
Oh she had a figure finer
Than the finest ocean liner
And unto her did I give chase

Next morning I awoke
My heart all torn and broke
No coat nor trousers could I find
But the judge he guilty found her
Cos she robbed a homeward-bounder
And she won't be down in Lime Street any more

Oh Maggie Maggie May
You won't be down in Lime Street any more
Cos she robbed so many sailors
And skint so many whalers
That she won't be down on Lime Street any more

This is a truncated version of the classic sailor's song of being robbed by a prostitute on returning to Blighty. Laurie says he learnt ditties like this from his time in the forces from 1942. Roud and Burton state that the song is first reported around the Mersey in 1757. A homeward-bounder is a sailor coming home from a long trip. Lime Street is in central Liverpool. In longer versions of the song other streets around the then-red-light district of Liverpool are mentioned. 'Canning Place' was a huge, Victorian sailors' lodging in Liverpool where the unfortunate matelot is presumably living and had received his pay for the voyage before meeting up with Maggie. The Beatles recorded a version of *Maggie May* on *Let it Be*.

5. *Goodbye Old Ship of Mine*

Laurie remembers this maudlin song being crooned by the old skippers on cold winter's days on the dumb barges. When he was acting as mate, for part of the journey Laurie was on deck holding hard to the tiller and getting as close to the chimney from the stove in the cabin for warmth. The skipper was down below in that snug cabin getting warm and eating some grub. When it came time for Laurie to go below for his food and warmth, and the skipper took his turn at the helm, this was one of the tunes that came down through the cabin hatch. First published in 1935, it has been recorded being sung before that in Gloucestershire as well as Yorkshire. The first verse is not always sung.

One day by the docks I was straying
By the quayside I happened to be
When I overheard someone saying
To an old ship just in from the sea

Goodbye old ship of mine
For no more we'll cross the line
Now your days are through
Sailing on the blue
So goodbye old ship of mine

When they break you up at dawn
In the yard where you were born
Oh they'll break a part
Of a poor sailor's heart
So goodbye old ship of mine

Your log book I'll keep as a token
In memory of you Mary Ann
I'd give the world to keep you
But I'm just a poor sailor man
So goodbye old ship of mine

And for the sake of Auld Lang Syne
Your name will still live on
Till the day that I am gone
So goodbye old ship of mine

GLOSSARY OF TERMS

Term	Meaning
Athwart	Across; normally used to describe a craft that has become stranded across the opening section of a bridge.
Battin' iron, lug, wedge	All used to make sure that the covers over the barge's hold are watertight. That's battening down.
Bed 'ole/bed side	Compartment above the cabin of the barge where the skipper slept. Usually on the starboard side.
Bight	A sharp bend in a river, or loop in a rope. Scott's Bight was one well-known example, lying between Selby Toll Bridge and the BOCM wharves.
Boathook	A long pole – around 20 foot – with a hook at one end and a pommel or pad for your shoulder at the other, used to manoeuvre a dumb barge around the docks.
Bucket elevator	A conveyor belt with grabs on the belt like a JCB's bucket. Used at BOCM to transfer loose seed or nuts from the barge's hold to the BOCM works. The cargo had to be shovelled into the buckets in the hold.
Bunker up	Fill with coal.
Clough	Pronounced in the Hull area as 'clew'. In other places it rhymes with 'plough'. A general term for openings in a lock such as paddles or sluices that are controlled to keep water at the desired level or to allow water to flow in or out.
Cob, cog or coggie boat	Small boat tied to the barge's stern, often used for sculling around the docks.
Cover	Weatherproof tarpaulin that went over the barge's holds. Often had to be battened down against the wind.
Derrick	Small crane either on-board or at a jetty or wharf to lift cargo between barge and dry land.
Dropping down	A term used at Selby when an empty dumb barge drifts, in a controlled way downstream on the ebb tide from the BOCM wharves at Barlby to the jetties in the centre of Selby.
Dujardin's Navy	Mr Dujardin was the general manager at the Selby mills in the 1930's. His 'navy' was the fleet of tugs and barges working between Hull and Selby. He's mentioned in the chorus of the 'SW&T' song.
Dumb barge	An unpowered cargo barge that had to be pulled up river by a tug, or moved around the docks with a boat hook.
Ebb tide	The flow of the river under gravity from Selby towards Hull. When the ebb is running and there is no 'fresh', the river level gradually gets shallower.
Flood tide	The surge of water upriver as the tide came in up the Humber. The 'flood' could travel at up to 8 knots, and reached as far inland as Naburn Lock. The flood rapidly increased the depth of water in the river.
Fore and afters	Supports running the length of the barge under the hatches.
Freeboard	The height of the barge deck above water.
Fresh	Extra water in the river on the ebb tide as a result of rainfall or snow melt in the upper part of the river catchment.
Gansey	A seamlessly-knitted tough, waterproof jersey.
Hanging off	Securing a cob boat or similar to the barge's stern.
Hoop	Another term for a sharp bend in the river.
Mooring head to tail	Barges moored in pairs, stern to bow, with anchors dropped so that they stand fast irrespective of the state of the tide.

Term	Meaning
Ness	A headland or point jutting into the river. The ness side of the river is the shallow side. Whitton Ness is one example.
Pen/penning	The pen is the chamber of water between the lock gates. Penning is to go in or out of a lock.
Pestering board	An extra length of wood fixed to the top of the cargo hold to increase its capacity, to allow a larger weight of 'light' seed to be taken on board.
Rack	A straight reach of river. Willow Tree Rack, just east of Selby was the site for singling out (qv).
Scuppers	Deck-level opening on barge to allow water to flow off the deck.
Selby Taurus	The Dews' family dumb barge (qv). The Selby fleet were named after celestial objects (see Appendix 1).
Shordnin'	The cry from the man wielding the depth pole if the river was becoming shallower as the barge crossed a sandbank.
Singling out	The procedure when dumb barges (qv) being towed as two pairs were re-arranged to be in a straight line of 4.
Slab cake	Cattle feed made from the leftovers of the seed after crushing. Often taken as a barge cargo back down river to Hull.
Slipping off the hook	Dying.
Snug	A barge well-filled with cargo, so likely to make a good profit.
Sounding rod/pole	Long pole - up to 20 feet - marked alternately black and white and used as a depth gauge.
Spare side	Opposite side of the cabin to the Bed 'ole. Usually the port side.
Staith(e)	Wharf where barges could moor and load/unload.
Steerage	The ability to manoeuvre a barge on the river. If you were going downstream with the tide, you had to be travelling at a faster rate than the tide to have steerage of the craft.
SW&T	'Selby Warehousing and Transport': the name given to the transportation arm of Soapy Joe Watson's Barlby business.
Telegraph	Device for delivering messages from the Bridge to the Engine Room on a tug.
Timber heads	Pronounced 'timmer 'eds', these are posts to which mooring lines could be made fast.
Towing hook	A post on the barge's stern to which tow ropes were attached.
W(h)arping line	Heavy duty rope attached to a drum on the barge, then fixed across a dock to allow craft to be pulled across the dock.

Appendix 4

THE LB CRAFT

Laurie's barge LBE.18 was part of the 36th Landing Barge Flotilla, which sailed from Chichester for Gold Beach under the command of Sub Lt Frank North RNVR.

Over a thousand such barges had been converted into craft for D Day in shipyards in both London and along the South Coast. Mainly powered by Chrysler marine engines provided as part of the U.S. lease-lend deal, the LBE's, had their stern "swims" removed and replaced with a large ramp operated by a hand winch. To beach the craft to deliver their load, the barges had to approach the shore stern-first, a difficult and dangerous operation in anything other than calm weather.

The D Day fleet contained all manner of support vessels, alongside those carrying the troops. They were all "LB's" of one form or another, the main categories being:

Landing Barge Emergency, or Emergency Repair, or Engineering, LBE - for maintenance and repair facilities for landing craft, including salvage. Equipped with stern ramp and carried workshop lorry (generator, lathe, drills, forge, anvil etc) which could be landed when needed or crawler crane for landing when possible. The LBE also carried its own generator, benches, welding & cutting equipment, forge & anvil, pumps, spare batteries etc and displayed a REPAIRS sign. Carried 150 or 200 tons. Their main armament was a 20mm Oerlikon. The crew was 1+9 deck/engine-room/maintenance, plus flotilla specialists up to total of 25. Each barge had an officer in command.

Landing Barge Oil, LBO - to supply diesel or petrol to coastal forces, landing craft, landing barges; refuelled from fuel tankers lying offshore. Equipped with cylindrical 40T/9,000 gallon capacity tank, two 5inch hand pumps, and displayed a DIESEL, PETROL, 73 OCT ('Pool' petrol), 87 OCT or 100 OCT sign. They did not have ramps. They carried 150 to 200 tons, and were armed with twin Lewis guns; crew of 5 including PO or L/S coxswain. LBOs were an unpopular posting as they were thought of as floating bombs, with (officially) no smoking on board at all times.

Landing Barge Water, LBW - to supply water to coastal forces, landing craft, landing barges; refuelled from water tankers lying offshore. Equipped with cylindrical 40ton/9,000 gallon capacity tank, two 5inch hand pumps, and displayed a WATER sign. They did not have a ramp. Carried 150 to 200 tons ; armed with twin Lewis guns; crew of 5 including PO or L/S coxswain

Landing Barge Kitchen, LBK - to provide prepared food, mainly for small landing craft. Large superstructure, equipped as galley to supply fresh bread and food equal to 1,600 hot and 800 cold meals daily; carried provisions to feed 900 men for one week. Not ramped, displayed a FOOD sign, Crew of 23. Sometimes armed with a stripped Lewis gun. Each barge had an officer in command - like most of the others, a sub lieutenant or midshipman RNVR. Also called "Bakeries", probably because of the smell of baking bread wafting across the water.

The 36th flotilla was one of ten such, consisting of 6 or 7 LBE, 10 LBO, 2 LBW, 1 LBK, 1 LCE,(Landing Craft Emergency Repair) and refuelling trawler.

With thanks to www.naval-history.net and www.6juin1944.com for this information.

BIBLIOGRAPHY

Books

Duckham, B.F.	*The Yorkshire Ouse*	David & Charles	1967
Farrah, H.	*Selby, The First 300 Million Years*		1987
Fletcher, H.	*A Life on the Humber*	Faber & Faber	1975
Geraghty, T.	*A North East Coast Town*		1945
Head, G.	*A Home Tour through the Manufacturing Districts of England*		1835
HMSO	*The Selby Bridge Act*	HMSO	1791
Lewis, S	*A Topographical Dictionary of England*	Lewis	1831
Morrell, W.W.	*The History and Antiquities of Selby*		
Mountain, J.	*A History of Selby : Ancient and Modern*		1800
Parsons, E.	*The Tourists' Companion*	Whittaker & Co	1835
Roud, S. & Bishop, J.	*New Penguin Book of Folk Songs*	Penguin	2012
Taylor, M.	*Dry Cargo Barges on the Humber Waterways*	History Press	2007
Taylor, M.	*Shipping on the Humber (The North Bank)*	History Press	2003
Taylor, M.	*The Yorkshire Ouse Navigation*	History Press	1988
Waite, A.	*Exploring the Yorkshire Ouse*	Countryside Books	1988

Other Publications

Gutteridge, P.	*Shipbuilding in Selby in the 19th century*	East Yorks Local History Society	2014
Selby Civic Society	*Swanning Around Selby*	Selby Civic Society	2014

Other items

Sam Dews' log book covering his work on the Ouse and Humber 1919–1934 (Unpublished, part of the Laurie Dews archive)

Research into the Dews' family tree (Unpublished, part of the Laurie Dews archive)

Archives of Selby Civic Society

Archives of Ye Olde Fraternitie of Selebians

Archives of the *Selby Times*

Archives of the *Goole Times*

Archives of the *Hull Daily Mail*

Archives of Hull Remembers/ Hull People's War

INDEX

Please note: References to Laurie Dews and his family, the rivers Ouse and Humber, the OCO/BOCM mills in Selby and the towns of Hull and Selby are so ubiquitous throughout the text that they have not been specifically referenced in this index.